The Gospe

The twelfth century's St. Bernard of Clairvaux likened a wise man to a reservoir that is deep and able to discharge the overflow without loss to itself. In his newest book, *The Gospel According to St. Bernard*, Bernie Brown discharges as a legacy to his grandchildren (and fortunately to us) the overflow of wisdom his reservoir has patiently been collecting for eighty years. This is a book to be treasured for its insight, love, passion, and forthrightness. Bernie states he wants to be remembered as a man who loved God and loved others. I submit he has already reached that goal.

– **Carol V. Aebersold**, coauthor of *The Elf on the Shelf: A Christmas Tradition*

Winston Churchill said, We make a living by what we get, but we make a life by what we give. In the case of my friend, Bernie Brown, he got much deserved recognition as the highly respected and innovative CEO of one of the largest nonprofit health systems in the country. Now retired, Bernie's life is focused on giving back. In this instance, he is sharing a lifetime of experiences with his grandchildren in *The Gospel According to St. Bernard*. It is more than a series of anecdotes. It is a road map on how to live a life of integrity, honor, joy, love, and faith. Not only his family but all of us are the beneficiaries of the wit and wisdom of this good man and a life well-lived.

– **Dick Yarbrough**, Georgia's most widely Syndicated Newspaper Columnist

Bernie Brown discusses the fact that we all live and function in different worlds. I don't know if there could be a better place to observe this than looking at a group of football players at a public high school. As a high school football coach, I am constantly looking for ways to reach and ultimately influence the players in a positive direction. Communicating effectively to this group who truly live and function in different worlds is not always an easy task. *The Gospel According to St. Bernard* is a great tool that can be used to spread wisdom and inspire self-reflection for not only young athletes but people of all ages! I'm excited for others to read and be influenced by Bernie's journey!

– **Gary Varner**, Head Football Coach, Allatoona High School, Acworth, Georgia, named Team of the Decade by the *Marietta Daily Journal*

Bernie and Snookie Brown are longtime family friends going back several generations. I am personally thankful for gentle and thoughtful men—like my own grandfather and like Bernie—who have a passion for imparting the wisdom of God to the next generations and passing down the teachings of the Bible to others (2 Timothy 2:2). Spending time building relationships, while sharing the gospel message, is the key to this. In a similar way, I view my own calling here in a university working with college students to be more of a Crock-Pot than a microwave ministry; it requires that kind of time and effort. I pray that, by God's grace, *The Gospel According to St. Bernard*, sharing eighty years of a Christian walk, will point others to the beauty of Jesus and the wisdom of God.

– **Andrew White**, Campus Director of Cru, University of North Carolina, Chapel Hill

THE GOSPEL ACCORDING TO
ST. BERNARD

Good News for the Grandkids from Pappy

Bernie Brown

Inspiring Voices

Copyright © 2020 Bernie Brown.

All rights reserved. No part of this book may be used or reproduced by any means, graphic, electronic, or mechanical, including photocopying, recording, taping or by any information storage retrieval system without the written permission of the author except in the case of brief quotations embodied in critical articles and reviews.

This book is a work of non-fiction. Unless otherwise noted, the author and the publisher make no explicit guarantees as to the accuracy of the information contained in this book and in some cases, names of people and places have been altered to protect their privacy.

Inspiring Voices books may be ordered through booksellers or by contacting:

Inspiring Voices
1663 Liberty Drive
Bloomington, IN 47403
www.inspiringvoices.com
1 (866) 697-5313

Because of the dynamic nature of the Internet, any web addresses or links contained in this book may have changed since publication and may no longer be valid. The views expressed in this work are solely those of the author and do not necessarily reflect the views of the publisher, and the publisher hereby disclaims any responsibility for them.

Any people depicted in stock imagery provided by Getty Images are models, and such images are being used for illustrative purposes only.
Certain stock imagery © Getty Images.

All Scripture quotations, unless otherwise indicated, are taken from the Holy Bible, New International Version®, NIV®. Copyright ©1973, 1978, 1984, 2011 by Biblica, Inc.™ Used by permission of Zondervan. All rights reserved worldwide. www.zondervan.comThe "NIV" and "New International Version" are trademarks registered in the United States Patent and Trademark Office by Biblica, Inc.™

Scripture quotations marked MSG are taken from THE MESSAGE, copyright © 1993, 2002, 2018 by Eugene H. Peterson. Used by permission of NavPress. All rights reserved. Represented by Tyndale House Publishers, a Division of Tyndale House Ministries.

ISBN: 978-1-4624-1301-0 (sc)
ISBN: 978-1-4624-1302-7 (e)

Library of Congress Control Number: 2020909550

Print information available on the last page.

Inspiring Voices rev. date: 05/21/2020

PROLOGUE

Pandemic

Most books do not have both a prologue and a preface, but I feel that something needs to be stated before we begin. The final draft of this book's manuscript was complete and being edited by the professionals when one of the most dramatic events in our lifetime occurred. Not only our country and communities but the entire world became infected with the coronavirus (Covid 19) resulting in a pandemic.

My world as well as yours was turned upside down as orders to "shelter in place" became prevalent. Businesses, schools and even churches were closed with basic activities being conducted online. It has been less than four months since the initial recognition of the seriousness of the situation. Our local newspaper reports over 2,000 cases and 100 deaths to date and mounting unemployment levels in the suburban county in which we reside. Almost all gatherings and events have been cancelled or postponed. Travel has been drastically curtailed, and "quarantine" has become a household term. Because of my age, I qualify as one who is "high risk."

At this point, my first thought was that publishing this book should be delayed to a better time when everyone was not so preoccupied and traumatized by the impact of this unbelievable turn of events. I asked some family members, friends and even the publisher for advice and then prayed for divine guidance. The answer came back loud and clear. I was told that the need for reassurance, hope, faith and love was never greater. Hopefully, this unique intergenerational work offers some of that and much more. "Good news" is needed and will be welcomed by those of all ages at a time such as this. Decision made – proceed with the release as soon as the editing, layout and production phases are complete.

I am now over eighty years old which should reflect a high degree of wisdom and maturity. However, when confronted with a seemingly overwhelming set of circumstances never faced before like the Covid 19 Pandemic, my mind tends to react more like an inexperienced child or youth. Each day has its moments of fear and panic. Then I remember the first Bible passage which I memorized that has sustained me for these many years. Back in those days, my Bible was The King James Version. It goes like this:

> *The Lord is my Shepherd, I shall not want. He maketh me to lie down in green pastures; he leadeth me beside the still waters. He restoreth my soul; he leadeth me in the paths of righteousness for his name's sake. Yea, though I walk through the valley of the shadow of death, I will fear no evil, for thou art with me; thy rod and thy staff, they comfort me.*
>
> *Thou preparest a table before me in the presence of mine enemies; thou anointest my head with oil; my cup runneth over. Surely goodness and mercy will follow me all the days of my life, and I will dwell in the house of the Lord forever.* (Psalm 23 KJV)

My prayer is that this modest literary effort will be helpful not only to my grandchildren but also to others who are hurting, discouraged and needy in any way.

– **Bernie Brown**

CONTENTS

Prologue v
Foreword xi
Preface xiii
Appreciation xvii
Introduction xix
An Open Letter to Each of My Grandchildren xxiii

Chapter 1 The Worlds of Life 1
              Life in Your Grandparents' World 3
              Life in Your Parents' World 4
              Life in Your World 6
              Life in God's World 8
Chapter 2 The ABC's of Life 14
              A—All 14
              B—Blessed 16
              C—Church 17
              D—Discipline 18
              E—Eternal 20
              F—Freedom 22
              G—Grace 23
              H—Hope 25
              I—Integrity 26
              J—Joy 28

	K—Know	30
	L—Love	31
	M—Me	33
	N—Name	34
	O—Obey	36
	P—Prayer	37
	Q—Quiet	39
	R—Righteous	41
	S—Seek	42
	T—Thanks	43
	U—Understanding	45
	V—Victory	47
	W—Wisdom	48
	X—Xmas	50
	Y—Yoke	51
	Z—Zeal	52
Chapter 3	Pappy's Will and Testimony	54
	Life in Sin or in the Son	55
	Stake in the Ground	57
	New Investment Strategy	58
	Family Mission Statement	59
	But for Four Inches	62
Chapter 4	Your Life and Decisions	64
Chapter 5	Summary and Conclusion	70

Epilogue: The Value of Old Folk	77
Family Album	81
Meet My Grandchildren	81
Family Photos	93
Notes	99

FOREWORD

Bernie Brown recently celebrated his eightieth birthday. In the days before our family gathered to honor him, I thought about what I could say about my husband that would embody my feelings in the short amount of time I would have to propose a toast. It was not until we passed around the sparkling grape juice to our children, grandchildren, and other guests that my mind began to clear. This is what I said:

> I want to be the first to raise my glass to the man I married fifty-seven years ago at the age of nineteen. If I had been writing a script for a marriage, I could not have chosen a more perfect leading man for the role of husband. I am the only one here who can give testimony to that fact, and I proclaim him the winner of the Superb Husband Academy Award. He's my man, but more importantly, he's God's man.

Bernie and I have raised three children together, and now we have achieved the status of grandparents with eight grandchildren and one great-grandchild. These children and grandchildren learned early on just how wise their "Pappy" is and never hesitate to lay their problems and life's questions at his feet. This literary effort is the culmination of Bernie's dream to reach out to these dear ones from a tangible record of a lifetime of learning. He especially feels a God-inspired nudge to share his Christian walk with them. He knows from experience in his personal spiritual growth just how much we all need a Savior. He does not want a single member of our family to go through this life without knowing Jesus Christ!

As Bernie's wife, I am his partner in all ways and his biggest fan. He calls me his "editor for life" and as such, I totally endorse this extraordinary message to our grandchildren. I guarantee that you will not want to miss reading any part of this "good news" coming straight from the heart of an eighty-year-old granddaddy.

Snookie Brown (a.k.a. Grammy)

PREFACE

All my grandchildren and now even my children call me Pappy. So to avoid confusion, just note that Bernie and Pappy are the same person. I value this affectionate title that was given to me at the birth of Lindsey, our first grandchild. I think it fits just right when coupled with the name given to Snookie, my wife. We stand tall when we are addressed as "Grammy and Pappy!" Today, we are proud parents of three plus their spouses, grandparents of eight, and great-grandparents of one so far.

In entitling these "scriptures" *The Gospel According to St. Bernard*, I feel the need to offer some explanation. In no way do I want this work to be viewed as presumptuous, aggrandizing, or sacrilegious. My dad was a preacher. His career, that followed his calling, spanned a period beginning in the 1930s and ending in the 1980s. He was a proponent of what was called in those days "old-time religion." He most often used New Testament scripture as basis for his sermons. Invariably, he would begin by reading the biblical reference and then state, "This is the gospel according to St. Matthew [or one of the other gospel writers]."

With this as background, let me explain my logic in selecting such a title. First, you may note that I called these *scriptures*. In this regard, please notice that I didn't capitalize this word. Here, these writings merely share some of my experiences that are of a sacred nature to me.

Second, when the word *gospel* is used, most will think of the four Gospels in the Bible (St. Matthew, St. Mark, St. Luke, and St. John). However, in the context of this work, I use the Old English definition of *god-spel*, which simply means "good news."

Third, you might believe that I'm claiming to be a *saint*. I am the furthest example of one who might have earned such a title. However, I do believe in the "communion of the saints," which refers to the members or parts of a single body headed by Jesus Christ. Therefore, although undeserving, I do claim membership in this body of believers.

Finally, let me give you my take on *St. Bernard* dogs. From what I've read and heard, they are large, lumbering, and lovable. Famous for rescuing lost travelers and skiers high in the Swiss Alps, these are giant dogs with a muscular frame and a friendly face—the sort of face you'd be grateful to see if you'd been stranded by an avalanche. However, you wouldn't be able to sip from the legendary barrel of brandy on their collars, because St. Bernards never wore them around their necks. These patient, unflappable dogs are fairly low maintenance, but they do enjoy plenty of company and several long walks a day. In regard to my having the attributes of this iconic animal, I humbly claim a few. I believe that I have a friendly face, and I'm low maintenance. I enjoy plenty of company and long walks with my wife. The other qualities are works in progress.

Simply put, I just want to share some "good news" with you that I have accumulated over the past eighty something years. Although you may believe that you don't need to be "rescued" from anything, that fact alone may make you a ripe recipient of these "scriptures." From a personal standpoint, I have learned that I cannot be found until I realize that I'm lost.

This probably will be my last attempt at book writing and may be the closest I will ever come to recording my spiritual autobiography. I pray that it might have value for family and friends who honor me by taking the time to read this modest effort to share from my heart.

Pappy/Bernie (a.k.a. St. Bernard)

APPRECIATION

In addition to my wife, my parents and siblings, my children and grandchildren, and all the others in my family who have loved and supported me for the past eighty years, I want to recognize and express appreciation to another group that has added spice and enjoyment to my life.

Since I have taken the liberty of identifying myself (St. Bernard) with those in the canine world, I want to give special thanks to my "granddogs" who lift my spirit and make me smile every time our paths cross. They include the following:

- Jenny and Marc Bailey's Ellie and Max
- Susan and Jeff Brown's Sammy, Louis, and Beau
- Amanda and Brad McLean's Gracie
- Amanda and Nathan Ward's Penny, Millie, and Conrad
- Brittany Bailey's Odette and Merce

I truly believe that relationships are among the greatest gifts that God has given us, even including those with different pedigrees. You can personally meet my granddogs in the "Family Album" at the end of the book.

INTRODUCTION

I began this literary effort with a heavy heart. It's Monday, February 18, 2019. We returned yesterday from a trip to Tennessee to attend the funeral of one of my sisters. My eightieth birthday will be toward the end of this year, and Suzanne was four years younger. In all, we have experienced the loss of nine members of our immediate and extended families in the past seven months, and all but two were younger than I am. These sorts of experiences cause one to not only do some soul-searching but also conduct a reevaluation of plans and goals for the rest of one's life. I am no exception.

Today, I am formally beginning an adventure—an effort to leave all that I can to those who come after me. My will and wishes concerning our small estate, including the distribution of various assets and items, are already in place. So you may ask, "What's left to pass on to your heirs and the next generation?" To that I would answer, "The important things!" However, I imagine that I'm probably like those who came before me who were worried about the world that their children and grandchildren would face. I'm usually an optimist, but now I often find myself thinking, *I'm glad that I'll be gone when all those projections and forecasts become reality. It's no doubt that most things in our society are worse than ever!* But is that true?

My guess is that the truth lies somewhere in between the extremes of optimism and pessimism. Do I have anything to offer that might make a difference in the lives of my family and love ones? I may not, yet I might. Therefore, I believe that the worst mistake in this regard is to fail to try.

Several years ago, I wrote a book entitled *Purpose in the Fourth Quarter: Finishing the Game of Life Victoriously*. In it, I reported on some informal research concerning the focus of each quarter of a person's life. My conclusions were as follows:

- first quarter: learning
- second quarter: earning
- halftime (midlife): crisis or commitment
- third quarter: discerning
- fourth quarter: yearning[1]

According to this, I am now in the "yearning" stage. Therefore, I am committing myself to take the challenge of yearning to make a difference. However, instead of wallowing in it with regrets, I hope to embrace this sense of yearning with enthusiastic vigor and offer some level of wisdom to those seeking victory in the game of life.

I will attempt to give organization to this effort to share my experiences and confessions. However, I'm by nature a storyteller and my grandchildren know this all too well. Some of my stories are good and some not so good. However, for a long time I did not realize that certain types of stories bring value above just a good laugh, a smile or a comment like "Oh Pappy." I once read that the more children know about their families' histories, the stronger their sense of control over their lives, the higher their self-esteem, and the more successfully they believe their families functioned. If you want to enrich family life, create, refine and retell the story of your family's best moments as well as the ability to overcome the difficult ones. That act alone may increase the odds that your family will thrive for many generations to come.[2]

Of course, storytelling carries the risk of overstating or

exaggerating my premises and points. So I ask you in advance to bear with me and even forgive my sometimes unintended distractions from my desire to be constructive and helpful. Hopefully, the lessons learned from this will be far more important than the tales that I have spun.

AN OPEN LETTER TO EACH OF MY GRANDCHILDREN

Dear Lindsey, Alex, Jordan, Noah, Nathan, Greta, Amanda, Brittany, and Ollie,*

Grammy and I just want you to know how much we love you and are so proud of the way you are growing and maturing into the persons we hoped you would become. You may remember us writing to you in the past on various occasions to let you know just how special you are to us.

This letter is a little different from past ones. Since you all are getting older and more mature, I feel that I'm writing to an older youth and young adult audience. So this is not a children's book but hopefully one that will be meaningful to you where each of you is now.

I still love and cherish you more than ever. And because of that, I feel at liberty to share with you some serious, heartfelt thoughts and ideas about ways to live to the fullest with purpose and meaning. God has a special and unique role for each of us to play in what I call the "game of life."

I feel that I may be uniquely qualified to share this with you for two reasons. First, I know you so well and love you so much. The day you became a part of my life, tears of joy flowed from my eyes and my heart was filled with love and thanksgiving.

Second, though I hate to admit it, I'm old and have seen and experienced a lot in the eighty years that I've been around. Also, you have always been kind and respectful to listen and make me think that my stories and tales were meaningful to you.

In the following chapters, I'm going to try to share with you some of the discoveries I have made in the "worlds" we live in. I say worlds because in a sense every individual is constantly faced with which world he or she wants to reside. Also, I would like to teach you the ABC's, and this time I don't mean the alphabet. I'm hoping that the "ABC's of life" will be interesting and helpful to you. In addition to these, I will share some very personal thoughts and hopes.

What you will find in these chapters are merely my observations collected over these many years. You may have a different perspective, but the important thing is that you begin giving serious thought and consideration in regard to the important life decisions you will face.

I love you now, and I will love you forever with all my heart!

May God bless you and keep you!

Pappy

*Ollie is our first great-grandchild.

CHAPTER 1

The Worlds of Life

When interacting with others, I sometimes wonder where they are coming from. Why can't they see that which is so obvious to me? On occasions, they not only disagree but are openly hostile to my thoughts and opinions. Interestingly, when I take time to stop and look at my own reactions, I realize that I too am at times in a retaliation mode toward them. Why is it this way?

The differences between us tend to drive us apart to the point that we retreat into an existence that makes us feel comfortable and secure. In my life, there are examples of estrangement between longtime friends and even relatives due to conflicting views on subjects and issues that are important to them. As a result, we tend to join the camp of the like-minded, which in itself further hardens the shell that we construct around ourselves. In analyzing the reasons for all of this, I sometimes wonder if we live and function in different worlds.

In an attempt to solve the riddle that causes brokenness and even hostile relationships, let's for the moment assume that different worlds do exist and that we are faced with choices with regard to the worlds in which to reside. If we accept this premise, it seems to me that the first step toward understanding is to define the worlds that are available for our inhabitance. Like most complex issues, there are many ways to seek an understanding of them; taking a historical approach is one. The following are addressed specifically to my grandchildren and are my attempt to do just that. These are some of the difference worlds inhabited by the generations that are still living today.

- your *grandparents'* world: the views from my generation
- your *parents'* world: the views about life the previous generation passed on to you
- your *own* world: the view that you currently have about life
- *God's* world: the view of the Creator's role in your life

As we attempt to explore the concept of different "worlds," we will need to think out of the box and in a true sense travel an unchartered course. I can recall often thinking that I live in a different world from many with whom I interact from time to time. Yet sometimes these same individuals and I seem to be on the same page regarding a particular issue. This has led me to conclude that we all may possibly travel in and out of several worlds in this game of life. To think in these terms, this concept becomes fascinating. If true, is this the right thing to do? Is it healthy for me to do this? Will I get lost? Is this a part of the game of life? And most importantly, is this consistent with God's plan for my life?

I realize that there are many ways to define the various "worlds" that exist, such as socioeconomic, racial, sexual, and even geographical. I have chosen a different one: generational. The fit is not perfect, but generally we can view this by exploring these past four generational groups commonly identified as Baby Boomers (1946–1964), Generation X (1965–1980), Millennials (1981–2000), and Generation Z (2001–). I have been told that children who know and appreciate their family origins and histories tend to be more successful in their pursuits. Remember this is directed

THE GOSPEL ACCORDING TO ST. BERNARD

to my grandchildren, whose ages range from lower teens to early thirties. Let's get started on this mini-history lesson.

🐾 LIFE IN YOUR GRANDPARENTS' WORLD

In identifying the world in which I was born (1939), I technically preceded the Baby Boomers by a few years. I was conceived by parents from what some term the "greatest generation." World War II was being fought and won, and they had survived the Great Depression. During this postwar period, the birth rate increased significantly. My dad was the first person in his family to go to college. He wanted to be a preacher, which required that higher educational pursuit. Even though we lived in one of the hottest places in the country (South Georgia), we had no air conditioning, and at one time, our home was heated only by a stove and fireplace. Telephones were shared with party lines that served several homes. I was a teenager before I saw a television show (black-and-white). Even the concepts of instant communication, cable television, cell phones, internet, and most of the other conveniences that we enjoy today did not yet exist. Very few families had more than one vehicle. Stuff had not become so important since we had very few resources to afford much. My first job was to deliver newspapers every morning in our neighborhood on my bicycle. I even collected from all my subscribers each week and paid the newspaper publisher I worked for. I was just twelve years old. We seldom locked our doors. All these types of things led to a much simpler, safer, and less complicated life for a kid like me.

One of the major ills of that time was racial segregation in most aspects of daily life. Much of this was established and enforced in our part of the country by state law. Thankfully, this began to change as the result of the civil rights movement. I remember my dad being asked, "What will we do if some blacks show up on Sunday at our worship service?" His answer was "They will worship with us!" This was not popular with some of the parishioners. Toward the end of my growing-up time, I began to sense major change in the air in society—some good and some bad. Focus toward self—particularly self-righteousness and self-centeredness—became more prevalent among this emerging group.

I can go on and on, but looking back, I grew up in a time that was wonderful in many ways. It was a time when marriage, family, and faith were the three most sacred and important aspects of life. By and large, having children was synonymous with marriage, and divorce rates were much lower. Discipline, behavior, values, and morals were taught and enforced by parents within the family unit. Most attended church, and stores were closed on Sunday. We knew our neighbors and loved our country. There were far fewer temptations and means of getting in trouble, and misbehavior did not carry the life or death consequences that it often does today. Let's start here and in today's terms call this the "conservative world." This was the world in which your grandparents grew up.

 LIFE IN YOUR PARENTS' WORLD

Your parents, my children, spent their early years during the Generation X era before being Millennials. Grammy and I moved fairly often during our first few years together. This resulted in our children being born in different states. In the previous generations, there was far less mobility with regard to work, so this created different challenges. Fortunately, I found my dream job earlier than most and now have lived in the same community for almost fifty years. This period may not have been the actual time of birth for the technological revolution, but many of the seeds for today's conveniences/necessities were planted then. My own manual typewriter was replaced by an electric one, and the early version of a computer was available on a limited scale. Credit became a means of purchasing not only major items like houses and cars but also just about everything else. This posed a very real problem for the undisciplined consumer.

Couples were older when they married; some even just lived together. In many cases, both parents worked outside the home, creating two-income households. Childcare and nanny services increased significantly as a result. Promiscuity and adulterous behavior became more common, and the divorce rate also began to climb. The abuse of drugs and alcohol became a serious health problem for the country. Mobility among this group grew with a great deal of migration from rural to urban and suburban areas (small towns to cities). The self or *me* attitude that had begun earlier continued to grow and flourish. A distinct emergence of individualism and self-sufficiency was obvious. The length of tenures in organizations tended to decline as individual interests took precedence over organization and institutional needs.

In comparison to the previous generation, fewer from this group regularly attended church and participated in civic/community affairs. Those who were members of churches generally chose one that had a contemporary style of music and worship. There is also a paradox here because some of the products of this generation are the most committed and fervent among the religious community. Interestingly, many institutions, such as government, education, entertainment, and some industries, quickly lead or embrace the cultural trends, be they good or bad. The nature of your parents' world has experienced enormous changes from the generation that preceded it. Therefore, in this context, let's call it the "transitional world."

🐾 LIFE IN YOUR WORLD

Where does an eighty-year-old granddaddy start describing, and how can he even comprehend the world of his grandchildren? In truth, he can only offer observations from the perch that he has occupied for many years. But maybe I'm reasonably qualified to offer an opinion because at one time I was where you are today. Then after Grammy and I had children (your parents), we watched them pass through the stage of life you currently occupy. Unfortunately, from my viewpoint, many trends that have been moving in the wrong direction are coming to fruition today in your world. In sharing my observations, I do not want you to view this in a hopeless way but with hope. I truly believe that we—you and I—can make a difference; I'll share some ideas concerning this later. The following are some of my thoughts and concerns that I admit are alarming:

Your world is high-speed. When something happens, we know it instantaneously, and unfortunately, often the facts are wrong or distorted. For instance, in traditional news as well as social media, speed to report and the desire to present an agenda often trump verified truth and accuracy. Therefore, many times we may be making decisions based on false assumptions.

Your world is prone to addiction and abuse. The availability of alcohol and illegal and prescription drugs, which began in previous generations, is now at an epidemic level. Additionally, inhaling addictions have expanded from just cigarettes to vaping and marijuana. Even food has become an addiction problem with obesity levels at a record high. The danger of these cannot be overstated. However, a new addiction medium that seems so innocent and even helpful is manifesting itself. They are called cell phones, tablets, and other technical devices. And it is unfortunate that such a small device can interfere with healthy relationships and, when used inappropriately, can even lead us into a world of darkness, despair, destruction, and danger. Recently, I was having lunch in one of my favorite restaurants. It was awfully quiet, so I looked around and only one of the tables was empty. The others were occupied with customers holding their phones in one hand and eating with the other. It was eerie. In my younger days, having a meal with friends was used primarily as our time to share and catch up. In the new age of social media, I have begun to worry that the best friends of many folks are their cell phones.

Your world is divided in many ways. Here are some examples: Democrat vs. Republican; conservative vs. liberal; traditional vs. progressive; urban vs. rural; men vs. women; old vs. young; employee vs. employer; and haves vs. have-nots. Depending on personal values and opinions, various components of our society tend to view this as good vs. evil. "My side is the good, and the other is evil." The proliferation of conflicting viewpoints tends to drive us further into what some call tribal warfare. All this fosters disrespect for and even hostility toward others.

Your world tends to blame its problems on society's ills rather than the lack of personal responsibilities. All this leads to disrespect for authority and justification for almost any misbehavior by individuals.

Your world has inherited many institutions that have lost their fundamental purpose and focus. Here are some examples: educational institutions neglecting basic skills while promoting social causes in their curriculum; human service providers placing more emphasis on the bottom line than serving and caring; and government, including its elected as well as employed officials, abandoning serving the people to maintain power and control over them. And even many of our churches have compromised truth to conform to societal values.

Your world is suffering greatly from the deterioration of families.

The family is probably the most critical institution to the well-being of any society, and it also has been detrimentally affected. Dysfunctional, abusive, and even loveless family situations seem to have become more the norm than the exception. Parental guidance and discipline have seemingly become a lost art in many situations. Unfortunately, recent surveys indicate that today's generation gives less value to family, faith, and patriotism than previous ones.

Before I close out this section, let me temper my observations; I don't want you to be discouraged and feel that I have abandoned my purpose for this little book: sharing "good news." First, let me say that most of these characteristics that I have described were not of your making. Instead, you inherited them from the generations that preceded you, including mine.

However, the most important thing that I could share with you is this: You don't have to conform to the world that you live in. Despite all this, you can become the person God intended for you to be. The world never has been and never will be perfect. If you view and react to these and many other challenges as opportunities, you can really make a positive difference. I know each of you well enough to anticipate that something good and special will result from your life. I predict that just before you complete your life here in this world, you will hear a still, small voice say, "Well done, good and faithful servant."

Keep reading. I've got some really good news next.

🐾 LIFE IN GOD'S WORLD

"Good news! Good news! Good news!" This is what Dr. Charles Sineath, my good friend and longtime minister, used to proclaim to get the entire congregation's attention for an important point at a critical time in his sermon. So let me begin this section by proclaiming, "Good news! Good news! Good news!"

In our life journeys, we all are faced with not only the question *where* but more importantly *how* we will live out our lives. Earlier in this chapter, we examined three different generational worlds that currently exist: your grandparents, your parents, and your world. Are we destined to reside in the one in which we were born, or can we claim a different address? I like, as well as dislike, certain features in each of them. But is there another option? I believe there is.

I hope that I have not bitten off more than I can chew while trying to explain what I'm calling "Life in God's world." I'm going to do my best to share a few key thoughts that I have discovered about this subject during these past eighty years. My first observation is that here we are talking about a *spiritual* world that has characteristics that are different from those that we are familiar with in our natural worlds. It also goes without saying that in order to understand God's world, we must first know some basic truths about God.

As we take a look at how the world is constantly changing with every generation, we can become very confused and frustrated about just how we should live. Most of us just take life as it comes, feeling that there's not much we can do about it anyway. I can make this statement honestly because I felt this way particularly in my early years. But as I have passed through the quarters of life (now in the late fourth quarter), I am becoming more aware that there is a plan available to us in "God's world" for *abundant* and even *eternal* living. And the enactment of that plan hinges on our willingness to undertake a spiritual treasure hunt to discover the key. Recently, while reading my regular morning devotional, which that day was entitled "Pay Attention to How You Live," I gained some insight into this puzzle. Let me share some of its points as well as some of my thoughts that were provoked from this short but intriguing article. This is the first paragraph:

What do you want out of life? Perhaps an even more challenging question is, 'What is it that consumes your thoughts, time, energy, and money?' As Christians, we live in two worlds—the earthly one and heavenly one. However, since the earthly realm is all we can see, it's easy to become sidetracked and begin living more for it than the spiritual realm into which we've been transferred by Jesus Christ.[3]

The scripture used as the basis for the devotional was from the Gospel according to Matthew.

> "Do not store up for yourselves treasures on earth, where moth and rust destroy, and where thieves break in and steal. But store up for yourselves treasures in heaven, where moth and rust do not destroy and where thieves do not break in and steal. For where your treasure is, there your heart will be also ... No one can serve two masters. Either he will hate one and love the other, or he will be devoted to the one and despise the other. You cannot serve both God and Money." Matthew (6:19-24)

Wow! I don't think that this told me anything that I didn't already know, but it did remind me of some very important things that I have a tendency to forget from time to time. My thoughts initially went to my treasury—first to my investment portfolio (money) and other tangible assets (stuff) where my financial wealth is recorded and then to my people (family, friends, and neighbors) where my personal treasures reside. If I am to reside in "God's world," in which of these two compartments should I invest the most time, effort, and resources to enhance or increase value?

THE GOSPEL ACCORDING TO ST. BERNARD

As I read the scripture, two experiences from long ago came to my mind. My first store-bought shirt was made of wool and was stored in a box in a closet during the hot summer months. When Mom got it back out for winter, it was severely damaged by moths. It was so special to me because it was a gift from a favorite aunt and uncle. Then, not too long after Grammy and I were married, my shotgun that I cherished, also a gift from a relative, was stolen from our home while we were on a church retreat. Such events remind us how fragile and even temporary ownership of earthly possessions can be. But we enjoy these things, and there is nothing wrong with that. However, do we place these *things* first in our house of treasures? Perhaps in life in God's world, there is a need for a "spiritual planner" with some guiding principles to help us change the focus of our investment strategies. Here are a few that I've learned that have helped me:

1. God created the world and we are here because of him, and most importantly, he loves us. If this is my Father's world, I believe that it is important get to know him better and seek his guidance. He is the owner, and we are temporary trustees of his world. We have an operating manual to help us—the Holy Bible—and a means to communicate with him: prayer.
2. He created each of us on purpose with a purpose. I have found that my purpose has changed as I have progressed through my four quarters. Our God-given gifts and talents will usually offer guidance in this regard. Discovering our purpose will help us know where to put our emphasis and efforts.
3. Willingness to take a chance or risk if we believe that we are following God's will is important. Stepping out of my comfort zone is not easy, but as we experience God's

guidance, the zone will widen beyond anything imaginable. A strong faith can overcome doubt and insecurity.

4. Follow his commandments, especially the two greatest ones: love God and love others. Remember God loved us first, so love him back. And he said that the best way to love him back is to love others—even an annoying brother or sister. Remember that love is not a feeling but an intentional action on your part. We believe in what we love.

5. Try to do our best in everything we do. We won't always be successful. But as my mother used to tell me, "When you do your best, angels in heaven can do no better."

6. Do not compare yourself with others. Doing this can be destructive and lead to envy and the inability to enjoy good relationships. You're not them, and they're not you. Another saying of my mother's was "Bloom where you are planted."

7. Always give thanks with a grateful heart. Probably nothing warms the heart of anyone, including God, more than a sincere, heartfelt thank-you. Thankfulness expressed is a gift to the giver.

Let me share one final thought. Our current senior pastor, Dr. Julie Boone, always closes our worship services by giving thanks to God, "the One who created us, redeems us, and sustains us." At first, I didn't give much thought to this benediction; it always sounded good. Then one day, it struck me that this is "life in God's world." As I have passed through the different quarters of life, the greatest changes in my life have been in "perspective." From early on, I knew that God was our *creator* (made us) and *sustainer* (provided for our needs). But I had not viewed him as a *redeemer* (saved us). I did not understand why we needed redemption. To do so is to admit being lost, fallen, or spiritually dead.

THE GOSPEL ACCORDING TO ST. BERNARD

A recent lesson series in my Sunday school class brought more clarity to me on this subject. Philip Yancey, in his book *Reaching for the Invisible God*, shares his perspective. A major theme that leads to reconciliation between us and God is the author's contention that "the World is good ... The World is fallen ... The World can be redeemed."[4] God created our world and saw that it was good. He gave the human race freedom, and we sinned, causing a separation from God that resulted in a fallen world. But the world can be redeemed by a Savior: the Son of God, whose name is Jesus.

Good news! Good news! Good news! So where will we reside, and how will we live? If we choose to follow God's plan, we will be *in* the world but not *of* the world. "*God so loved the world that he gave his one and only son, that whoever believes in him shall not perish but have eternal life*" (John 3:16).

I have a ton more gospel lessons to share, which will assist if we wish to spend our lives in God's world. Remember the definition of gospel is "good news." In this regard, I hope that you find more good news in the next chapter, where I share my ideas on the ABC's of life.

God loves you, and I love you too.

This is the gospel according to St. Bernard.

CHAPTER 2

The ABC's of Life

I can still remember my mom making me practice my ABC's. I would soon be in school, and she wanted me to be a good student and successful in my academic pursuits. To be honest, I wasn't the least bit interested in much of anything except playing, eating, and sleeping. However, without her persistence, I doubt that I would have survived, much less been successful in my studies. The ABC's soon became words, words became sentences, and sentences became paragraphs. And in certain cases, reading even became fun; a new world opened up for me.

Could it be that a similar exercise can be applied in assisting us with our desire to have a good life and be successful in its pursuit? Let's give it a try by selecting and examining a key word that begins with each letter of the alphabet. These are mine, and I share them with you in an effort to inspire and motivate you to develop your own ABC's of life.

 A—ALL

A: There are so many good words to select from, but I picked *all*.

THE GOSPEL ACCORDING TO ST. BERNARD

> In answer to the question, *Teacher, which is the greatest commandment in the law, Jesus replied: "Love the Lord your God with all your heart ..."* (Matthew 22:36-37)

Wow! How do we love with all our hearts? I've been practicing and I'm not perfect, but I'm getting better at it. I think it started with my mom and dad and then the rest of my family (it was a little harder with sisters). But I really began to understand the true meaning of "Love ... with all your heart" when I met Grammy. She was the cutest and most beautiful girl I had ever seen. It may not have been at first sight, but very soon afterward, I was in love. Counting courting, engagement time, and our married life, we are approaching sixty years together. I loved her from the beginning, but the more I got to know her, the more I loved her. I truly love her with all my heart, and she loves me with all her heart; we tell each other that often. Could it be that we need to spend time with the Lord and get to know him better in order to truly love him with all our heart? It should not be that hard, if we realize that his Spirit already resides in our hearts just waiting on our decision to recognize his presence. Interestingly, my love for Grammy has grown so much because the Lord showed me by his example that he loved me with "all [his] heart"!

I have one afterthought in regard to "all." This morning, I attended a worship service at my church that was led by the youth. The music was theirs—very contemporary with guitars and other band instruments. There were also some ritual aspects included in a more tradition style. I would call the service blended. But what made it so meaningful to me were the messages delivered by four high school students. The common title of their remarks was "All in!" Individually, they gave their testimonies and explained their commitment to the Lord Jesus Christ!

Think on this: I truly believed that we are "all in" by going "all out."

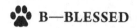 B—BLESSED

B: This letter also has some good choices, but *blessed* kept rising to the top. I guess it's because I feel truly blessed!

> <u>Blessed</u> are the poor in spirit ... those who morn ... the meek ... those who hunger and thirst for righteousness ... the merciful ... the pure in heart ... the peacemakers ... those who are persecuted because of righteousness ... (Matthew 5:2–12)

The word "blessed" comes to mind when a few of my friends, when asked how they are doing, will answer, "I'm blessed!" The answering machine message of Frank, my brother-in-law, ends with "Have a blessed day." Often, we think of a gift, a feeling, happiness, a wonderful state of being and even something holy when this word is used. These are all true, but from where and when do blessings come? In my experience, it seems to be the result of something a person does or who that person is. I've always been told that it is more blessed to give than to receive and to get a good night's sleep, count your blessings instead of sheep. I overheard Earl, another of my brothers-in-law, instruct a waiter to bring him the check for the meals of a couple of soldiers sitting across the dining room. He made sure that we had left before the recipients of his generosity were informed. Earl was blessed, the two soldiers were blessed, and I was blessed to witness the whole thing.

Often we do not even recognize how blessed we are until a period of time has passed following certain events. On one occasion, I remember the disappointment of missing a job opportunity to discover a short time later that I was being considered for something much better. Though we from time to time may be on the giving or receiving end, we need to remember to "praise God from whom all blessings flow!"

Think on this: some view good things as luck; I see them as blessings.

🐾 C—CHURCH

C: The word I chose here has played a significant role in my life; *church* has been like a second home.

> *And he (Jesus) is the head of the body, the <u>church</u> ...*
> *(Colossians 1:18)*

I belong to a unique "fraternity." I'm a PK, which stands for "preacher's kid." My home until I left to go to an out-of-state university was a parsonage owned and provided by the church. Only a few pieces of furniture actually belonged to my parents. The table where we ate, the sofa where we sat, and even the bed where I slept were not ours. They were there when we came and when we left. The system of appointing pastors at that time generally dictated a move every four to five years. My upbringing thus was in five different parsonages. I share this to emphasize how significant the church has been in my life back then and also now.

We are told that Jesus is the head of the church and the church is a body made of many parts (believers). Working together, this body (institution) can be a powerful force and instrument for good in our world. Being an organization-oriented person for my entire professional career, I am intrigued with God's plan for organizational effectiveness. He made Jesus the CEO and has a special position for each of us in the hierarchy of the church. If you are like me, you probably want to be as high up on the chart as possible. Am I to be an eye to see needs, an ear to hear cries, a hand to encourage, an arm to lift a burden, a leg to run, or maybe the ultimate: a heart to care? Lord, let me be someone who's important in the kingdom.

But what if my assignment was to be the heel: the very lowest part of this magnificent body the church? What a put-down! Nobody will see me, and most won't even know that I exist.

Let me give you another perspective of this. I have known three men who accidentally fell and crushed or fractured their heels. The pain was relentless, the recovery was slow, and the rehabilitation was intense. They could hardly get around without a wheelchair, a scooter, crutches, etc. for an extended time. Without the heel, the body loses its balance. From this, I learned that the heel supports the foot, the foot the legs, the legs the back, the back the arms, shoulders, and neck. When Jesus told Peter that he would be the rock on which the church would stand, I couldn't help but think, *On that rock sits the heel of the church giving it balance.* It's interesting how God views the body of Christ. The top shall be the bottom and the bottom shall be the top. Jesus came to serve and not to be served. He just turned the organization chart upside down to make sure we realize that all our roles in the church are important.

Think on this: remember that church is made up of sinners who have been forgiven.

🐾 D—DISCIPLINE

D: I have learned that there are two types of *discipline:* external and internal.

> *He who heeds <u>discipline</u> shows the way to life ...*
> (Proverbs 10:17)

When I think of the word *discipline,* my thoughts immediately

THE GOSPEL ACCORDING TO ST. BERNARD

go back to when I was a kid. My misbehavior almost always led to some type of discipline through punishment administered by my parents, teachers, or coaches. Looking back, I don't feel like I was abused in any way. Actually, I probably got off lightly for most of my wrongdoings. Now I realize how much the discipline that I experienced under those who were responsible for me and my upbringing helped shape who I am today. Discipline taught me how to study and learn, how to be responsible for my actions, how to stay out of trouble most of the time, and even how to clean my room and do so many more of life's lessons. It may have even saved my life a time or two. There even were a few times when I had a positive influence on some of my buddies from some of the lessons that I had learned. This early form of discipline was enforced by individuals who had jurisdiction over me in various venues. I consider this "external" discipline.

Then the day came when I was gradually freed from the various authorities under whom I was raised. When I went off to college, I had no one to wake me up, prepare my meals, and remind me of the deadlines that must be met plus all the other responsibilities of being on your own. I then got my first job as a professional, got married and had a family, and became a part of a community. These life experiences were full of ups and downs, wins and losses, rights and wrongs, and bests and worsts. And of course, there were all sorts of temptations. Looking back, what I needed most during those times was guidance like I had had when young that would bring order and discipline to my life. But where could I find it?

It was not an instant revelation but probably an evolutionary process that led to a significant discovery. Discipline need not result only from external sources but also may be claimed from internal fortitude. Interestingly, I learned that many of the principles, including discipline, that were imbedded in me from my childhood were still there and could be accessed when needed. Things like integrity, honestly, sharing, serving, caring, and love, among many other characteristics, still helped guide my life.

However, the most important discovery that I made concerning internal discipline was this: I still have a counselor who is always available and can guide me in my decisions, desires, and even the purpose for which I exist. When Jesus was crucified, resurrected, and returned to heaven, he left someone to remain to counsel and guide us thought our life's journey. To be honest, it was a bit later when I truly discovered this fact, even though I had heard about him all my life. He is called the Holy Spirit and is part of the Trinity. He has now been in my life for many years and resides in my heart. If you haven't discovered and invited him into your heart yet, I highly recommend you do it as soon as possible. He is available to everyone. I believe in God the Father, God the Son, and God the Holy Spirit.

Think on this: a truly disciplined person under the guidance of the Holy Spirit is called a *disciple*.

 E—ETERNAL

E: This word *eternal* is one that we need to think about more.

> For God so loved the world that he gave his one and only son, that whoever believes in him shall not perish but have <u>eternal</u> life. (John 3:16)

Life can be so demanding in our busy world with schoolwork, job work, homework, volunteer work, and even church work. With deadlines, complications, interferences, and other endless challenges, how can we think beyond today? Maybe now and then we can look ahead to a few tomorrows. But when do we have the time or even the energy to give thought to eternity?

THE GOSPEL ACCORDING TO ST. BERNARD

To complicate things even more, we can get addicted to so many things in the world that seem so innocent but further capture our time and energy. Many of these are habits that are not evil or destructive in themselves, but the excesses they bring are continual sources of distraction from the true and best purpose for our lives.

One day I was watching an evangelist on television. He was one of those who walks around when delivering his sermon. I noticed that he had a long, attached rope trailing him as he went from one side to the other in the pulpit area. The rope was distracting, but I couldn't seem to change channels. I hoped that some explanation would come out about this strange behavior. At the very end of his sermon, he gathered up the rope, which looked about twelve to fifteen feet long. At one end of the rope was about an inch of tape wrapped around it—like you might think was there to keep the rope from unraveling. The preacher then gave an explanation of this unusual prop. He indicated that the small inch of rope that was taped represented our time here on earth. And the balance of the rope was symbolic of eternity. He noted that typically our focus and energy were relatively just the opposite; more than 99 percent on now and less than 1 percent on eternal things. I don't remember a single point that he made in his sermon, but I will never forget the point that he drove home in this illustration. I even used it once when it was my turn to teach our Sunday school class.

A few years ago, probably because we are getting older, Grammy and I decided to look at the different charities, including our church and other ministries that we had supported. We prioritized them in regard to what they contribute to others and as a result have changed some of our giving. The top ranking was given to those organizations, programs, and ministries that bring the highest eternal value. Much of this is centered on telling about God giving his Son, Jesus, to take away our sins. And believing in him, we shall not perish but have eternal life.

Think on this: Eternal life is forever. Don't let the distractions or even the pleasures of today deter you from the relationship that leads to eternal life!

 F—FREEDOM

F: I chose this word because *freedom's* ramifications are much like a two-edged sword.

> *Exercise your <u>freedom</u> by serving God, not by breaking the rules.* (1 Peter 2:16 The Message)

When one has freedom or free will, the implication is that person has the ability to make choices. It is fascinating to me that God, who can do anything, chose to give us the freedom to make our own decisions or choices. As a result, this gives us the ability to accept or reject his will, purpose, laws, and rules for our lives. With this freedom come consequences that can range from marvelous to disastrous. Interestingly, if we weren't given this freedom and were just programmed to always know and do the right thing, we would be no more than robots. I guess that God wanted children rather than robots as his chosen ones.

I share this with you because it may explain in a general way why we can't understand much that is going on in our world today. In the recent past, two of my friends were killed in separate automobile accidents shortly after retiring from jobs that provided tremendous public service to our community. Some years ago, the son of one of my close friends committed suicide. A rookie policeman was killed trying to protect others. A young, talented athlete was paralyzed as the result of a freak vehicle accident. The marriage of two of the most committed servants that I know is coming to an end. The murder and crime rate in one of our major cities makes it appear a war zone. A recent hurricane devastated an island community. It's depressing to watch the news because it's mostly bad! Could it be that we live in a fallen world?

Why is it that bad things happen to good people, and conversely, why can good things happen to bad people? I certainly don't know the answer, but I do believe that many things that happen are the result of choices made by people exercising their God-given freedom. And unfortunately, my bad choice can affect others and theirs can affect me.

Some good news here! I'm going to continue to trust in almighty God, who loved me so much that he gave his only Son. Through faith, I can think of no better choice than this as I exercise my freedom!

Think on this: freedom brings choices; think before making them!

🐾 G—GRACE

G: I felt that there were two great choices but ultimately selected *grace* without abandoning my other possibility. I'll explain this later.

> But just as you excel in everything—in faith, in speech, in knowledge, in complete earnestness and in your love for us—see that you also excel in this <u>grace</u> of giving.
> (2 Corinthians 2:7)

The definition of the word "grace" that I usually hear quoted is "unmerited favor" or, stated another way, "receiving something good that you didn't even deserve." This concept is somewhat counter to the lessons that our worldly culture teaches. We are told that we must earn our way to success, or in the marketplace, we must eat what we kill, or we will only receive what is earned and deserved. Certainly, some of this is good. We need to be responsible and hopefully successful in our search for purpose and meaning. But I am truly *grateful for grace* that carries me when I falter or fail, when I miss the target, or when I am discouraged or overwhelmed. I'm reminded of this when we sing one of my very favorite hymns. It says,

> Amazing Grace! How sweet the sound—That saved a wretch like me! I once was lost but now am found, was blind but now I see. The Lord has promised good to me, His word my hope secures; He will my shield and portion be as long as life endures.[5]

The other G word that I thought would be a good one was *gift*. Then, when I began to think more deeply about these two words, I realized that grace and gift have much in common. Actually, grace is a gift. In my mind, grace is that amazing gift that God gave me. But the scripture above places this in a different light. As we seek to be successful in our lives through the grace of God, we are reminded to not forget to "also excel in this grace of giving" to others. Could it be that as we receive God's amazing grace, we need to pass it on to others? In so doing, they will not only receive the blessing of the gift of grace from us but will also be introduced to God's grace.

I believe that God's command to us as believers can be boiled down to a primary one that is evident here: be gracious givers while earnestly practicing our faith, speaking words of wisdom and encouragement, sharing the truths we know, and loving others.

Grace can truly be a lifestyle that reflects God's favor and love toward us. To recognize that fact is noble; to share it with others is divine.

Think on this: accept God's grace gracefully, and then gracefully share it!

 H—HOPE

Hope: What would life be without *hope?* Not much, in my opinion.

> *We have this <u>hope</u> as an anchor for the soul, firm and secure.* (Hebrews 6:19)

Hope is a big part of my Christian walk. However, I remember often using the word "hope" very loosely in my worldly vocabulary. "Bernie, are your grades going to be better this semester?" Daddy would ask. "I hope so," I would answer.

"I hope I can," "I hope not," "I hope she likes me," and "I'm hoping for the best but preparing for the worst" are a few more of my normal statements. But when I began to get serious about my relationship with God, I kept hearing the word "hope" used often and with a different meaning. For example, in the Bible, it stated, *"And now these three remain: faith, hope and love"* (1 Corinthians 13:13). For hope to be included with faith and love meant to me that hope should be something I should embrace.

A Christian's definition of hope is far better than the world's. In this context, hope is like faith that cannot be changed by circumstances or what the eyes see because an unseen God is seen in his faithfulness. In this world, I cannot imagine living without something in which to have faith, trust, and hope. I certainly don't trust myself to be my guide through this scary, sometime hopeless world.

An experience in regard to a personal habit gave me insight into what hope really should be. Every morning for years, I began my activities of the day doing two things: having my devotional time, including Bible study, and then reading the local newspaper that is delivered to our home. At first, my pattern was to get the spiritual stuff (like faith, hope, and love) out of the way as quickly as possible. Then I could read the more interesting newspaper from cover to cover. As a result, I didn't seem to be making any headway into growth of my faith.

Then one day, disappointingly the paper wasn't delivered due to a tree falling across our road. So I just filled up my time reading more closely the devotional and more of the biblical references. I don't now think that it was coincidental that the day went better than usual with my mind remembering some of the lessons from my expanded study. Soon afterward, I was asked to teach a Sunday school class, which required even more in-depth study and preparation. As a result of this, I now spend all my time at the breakfast table in God's Word and find time later to read the paper.

I was thinking about how my morning habits had changed and the positive impact that this had on my life. Then I realized what was happening. I was rushing through my Bible study and therefore missing a tremendous amount of "good news" that brought *hope* into my daily activities. Then I would spend most of my time with the newspaper that unfortunately was largely filled with the day's "bad news" that often left me feeling *hopeless* and discouraged as I faced my day. I once heard that God's definition of hope is not a "hope so" but a "know so."

Think on this: you can live approximately forty days without food, three days without water, four minutes without air, but not one second without hope.

🐾 I—INTEGRITY

I: If the world needs more people with *integrity*, where can we find them?

> And he still maintains his <u>integrity</u>, though you incited
> me against him to ruin him without any reason.
> (Job 2:3)

THE GOSPEL ACCORDING TO ST. BERNARD

To be called a man or woman of integrity is about the highest compliment that one can receive. When hearing this concerning someone, my mind goes to words like *honest, trustworthy,* and *noble*. But how does this play out in practical terms? Does living a life defined by integrity pay off? Let me share a simple example that demonstrated this asset in one's life that impressed me in a powerful way. To be honest, if the shoe was on the other foot, I'm not sure that I would have risen to this level of integrity. Please forgive me if I get too graphic and personal.

A few years before I retired, I was having some dental issues. I blame this on the fact that I grew up before fluoride became standard in all toothpaste. My mouth was full of fillings and discolored teeth. My dentist had done the best he could with what he had to work with. Finally, he said, "Bernie, I think you need to have crowns put on all your upper front teeth." Almost all my back teeth already had crowns added over a long period of time, and they were less obvious. The cost to do this all at once for the eight teeth just about blew my mind. I had a dental insurance policy, but that would cover only a very small portion of the cost. With Grammy's encouragement and the desire to be able to smile without being self-conscious for the rest of my life, I proceeded to have it done. I felt like a new man, and to this day, I believe that this was one of the best investments that I've ever made.

At least five years later, I noticed that part of the back of one of the crowns had a rough place on it. I could feel it with my tongue. At my next visit to the dentist several months later, he checked it out and found a small piece of the tooth had cracked off. He also identified two more adjacent ones were also cracked. The bottom line was that all these could not be repaired but would need to be replaced. To make this more traumatic, I no longer had dental insurance that had been provided by my former employer.

The whole situation was especially awkward because my

original dentist had retired and my new dentist had taken over his practice within the group. When I came for the scheduled appointment to begin the replacement process, I asked Brian about a payment plan to cover this. Without any hesitation or second thought, he said, "There will be no charge for this." I told him that would not be right. I may have bitten down on something hard causing the fractures. He would be covering the cost of something that happened before he was here. I even offered to share the cost, but he would not budge from his stance on this. If I had not brought up the subject of money, it probably would have never been mentioned.

This experience was not the only reason that I knew my new dentist was a man of integrity. It had begun long before this incident. You see, Jim, the dentist who preceded him was a man of integrity I have known and admired for many, many years. He wouldn't have allowed his practice to be taken over by anyone who was not of the highest integrity. And now, having known Brian for many years, I can see that his values, his priorities, and his faith are of a man with the highest integrity.

Think on this: integrity begins in a person's heart in private before it is exhibited in public.

J—JOY

J: This is one of my very favorite words. The best days of our lives are when we embrace *joy*.

> *I have told you this so that my joy may be in you and that your joy may be complete.* (John 15:11)

Often when greeted by others, they ask, "Are you doing okay?" And most answers are something like this: "Yes, I'm doing fine."

THE GOSPEL ACCORDING TO ST. BERNARD

This has always bothered me because I want to be more than okay or fine. Unless I'm have an unusually hard day, I usually answer, "No, I'm not doing okay. I'm doing great!" Exchanges like this have led me to conclude that there is a difference between how we feel and how we truly are.

If we have a choice, I believe that the best state in which to be is that of joy. Grammy and I have a friend we have known for many years. Before her husband died a while back, we did some things together as couples. Additionally, over the years, she has experienced some very serious injuries and illnesses that have limited her capabilities and thus many of her activities. We don't see her as much as we used to, but every time we cross paths, she is upbeat, smiling, and filled with enthusiasm. She may be one of the most contagiously positive and joyful persons I have ever known. Interestingly, it doesn't take long to understand why she is such a special person in this regard. I have never asked her about her attitude and approach to life. However, those of us who know her have concluded that it's fairly simple. You see, her name is Joy, and she is committed to living up to her name. And you know, every time I see her, I'm filled with joy also.

Here are the words from a popular song written over thirty years ago:

> Here's a little song I wrote you might want to sing it note for note.
>
> Don't worry, be happy!
>
> In every life we have some trouble but when you worry you make it double.
>
> Don't worry, be happy!

Don't worry, be happy now![6]

Some like to distinguish the difference in happy and joy. Happiness is viewed as a feeling, and joyfulness is an intentional mind-set. There may be some validity in this, but in my mind, the goal we all should seek is to live a life filled with joy, irrespective of circumstances.

The scripture above gives a clue to experiencing joy. Open your Bible and read what comes after that verse (John 15:12–13). In my Bible, the words are in red letters, which means Jesus said them.

Think of this: joy is not a happening; it's your response to it.

🐾 K—KNOW

K: A friend of mine often would say, "When you *know* it in your knower, you *know* it." That's why I knew that I must select *know*.

> The man who thinks he knows something does not yet <u>know</u> as he ought to <u>know</u>. But the man who loves God is known by God. (1 Corinthians 8:2–3)

I remember hearing old folks say, "It just seems like the older I get, the less I know." This didn't make a lot of sense to me until recently. At my age, coupled with advancements in technology and other types of basic knowledge, I just can't keep up and process it all. What about all this? Am I less qualified to exist and have a meaningful life in this world because of my diminishing knowledge base? I hope not, and I honestly don't think that life is over. To the contrary, I don't remember being more energized with a sense of purpose and meaning.

In light of all this, I seem to be coming back to a simple question: what do I really need to know? Just before the verse from

1 Corinthians stated above, it says, *"We know that we all possess knowledge. Knowledge puffs up, but love builds up."* (1 Corinthians 8:1) Is this saying that knowledge is not important? I don't think that's what it means. Actually, the word *know* is used 203 times in the Bible. I know that all this can get confusing, so let me take a shot at simplifying it. I believe that you don't have to know everything but instead just a few important things.

Knowledge resides in our brains just like data is stored in a computer. The way that I typically access that data is by going to the program where it is stored and entering my password. Could it be that the important things of life that we need to know are always available to us if we know where to go and have a password? One's mind is like a computer, but it has much greater capacity because it is connected directly to a body that can respond and follow directions. But more importantly, there is a heart that can override the dictates of the mind to ensure the actions prescribed are appropriate, moral, and good. The heart is connected to the Creator through a Holy Spirit that resides there. However, it can only work properly if *we are known by him*. But what is the password? This is it: write it down in your mind and heart. It is *love*. Read the scripture again; it was there all the time. "But the man (or woman) who *loves* God is known by God."

I believe this with all my heart because "when I know it in my knower, I truly know it."

Think on this: remember your password, and use it often.

🐾 L—LOVE

L: This word had to be included because *love* is one of the most used words in the Bible.

And the second is like it: "Love your neighbor as yourself." (Matthew 22:39)

Just before this verse indicating the second most important commandment is the greatest commandment: *"Love the Lord your God with all your heart and with all your soul and with all your mind."* (Matthew 22:37) In reading this, I am impressed that it mentions love for three individuals. First, love God, then love your neighbor, and also love yourself. Let's take these three one at a time in reverse order.

Love to me is the highest level of affection toward someone or something. Love includes eagerness and enthusiasm, and it is hard to keep it from showing. I believe that love first starts with love of self. As babies, our initial needs and demands, and therefore our focus, are on ourselves. Very soon afterward, we meet our first neighbors, our mother, father, or caregiver. And as a result, we learn to love others. The final revelation (love God) comes later to us. It's probably impossible to love someone whom you do not know. Therefore, it is imperative that someone introduce us to our Creator, the Almighty God. All three of these relationships are very personal and individual in nature. It is interesting and helpful to hear each other's love stories, but I have never heard a single one that is identical to mine.

Unfortunately, our love life can become distorted and misdirected. A disproportional love of self, mistaking lust or some evil folly for love, too much love toward things, or simply omitting one of those whom we are commanded to love are examples of the way our love life can go awry. Another stumbling block is the fact that we often believe that love is a feeling. I learned in a marriage retreat many years ago that true love is not a *feeling*; instead it is an *action*. Certainly, both feelings and actions are part of our love experience—when both giving and receiving. This is important because feelings can be fickle but acts of love are intentional. I have come to realize that love expressed by my actions is the most meaningful. Feelings then often follow. This discovery has enriched my life.

At my father's funeral over thirty years ago, a pastor friend of ours told me something that inspired and made me want to be like Dad. He said, "I have never known anyone who loved to love others as much as your dad."

Think on this: I love each of you and God does too! And don't forget it!

 M—ME

M: Selecting *me* in this case allowed *me* to look at a well-known story from a different viewpoint.

> *The younger one said to his father, "Father, give <u>me</u> my share of the estate" ... The older brother became angry ... "I've been slaving for you and never disobeyed your orders. Yet you never gave <u>me</u> even a young goat."*
> (Luke 15:12–32 excerpts)

There's a story in the Bible about a prodigal son (and a resentful son). The younger of two sons asked their father to give him the share of the property now, which would normally past to him when the father died. The father gave the son his share of the inheritance, and he in turn squandered it in a foreign land. When all was gone, this son sent word that he wished to come home and just have the job of a servant for his father. But the father welcomed him home with open arms and a loving heart. Seeing this, the older brother was infuriated and resentful because he had remained loyal to his father and never received this much attention.

I always thought that this was a neat parable about a rebellious and irresponsible son and his brother, who was justifiably resentful and unforgiving. But this story didn't have anything to do with me. I had not taken any money and wasted it. Of course, there was not much to take since my family was probably in a lower income bracket and never owned our own home. We were rich but not in things. And I haven't been resentful of my sisters; I don't have a brother. Actually, I couldn't even think of any of my friends who fit the mold described in this story.

Then one day through one of those mysterious ways God speaks to us, I felt a nudge to look more deeply at this parable. The greatest wealth that any of us can receive doesn't come in the form of earthly possessions but from a treasure house under the control of a loving heavenly Father. So the lesson in this story for each of us is this: First, there is a great inheritance awaiting those who believe and place their trust in God, and we should not let it be wasted. And second, our role is not to judge or convict our brothers or sisters for their actions; that's God's job. Our human traits toward squandering and resenting are tendencies that we should make every effort to avoid. But fortunately, when invariably these do occur, remember that we have a forgiving and loving Father who takes us back and welcomes us home.

Think on this: primarily focusing on what is in it for *me* will bring disappointment, whereas placing importance on handling *my* treasure responsibly and relating to *my* brothers and sisters lovingly will bring peace and joy.

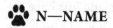 **N—NAME**

N: I chose *name* because we sometimes forget just how important a good one is.

THE GOSPEL ACCORDING TO ST. BERNARD

A good _name_ is more desirable than great riches; to be esteemed is better than silver or gold. (Proverbs 22:1)

My full name is Bernard Loam Brown Jr. My dad was Bernard Loam Brown Sr., which means that I was named for my father. It's interesting to research the origin and meaning of one's name. In my case, I found that "Bernard" means strong, brave bear, "Loam" is a rich soil mixture, and "Brown," which has an English/Scottish origin, is the fourth most popular last name in our country. Currently, the most famous person having the same last name is Charlie Brown. Of course, Bernie is the nickname for Bernard. That name has been used much more recently because of a fellow running for president of the United States.

History and ancestry are interesting, but when a name is called, what do others think? Usually, when I hear the name of someone that I know, my mind immediately envisions that individual. I have an opinion based on my relationship and interaction with that person. The names of my good friends carry very high ratings; those that I know by reputation for integrity and honesty also are highly ranked. And then there are a few that are off the scale because of the love that we have for each other that has developed over many years. For example, when I hear the name Snookie, a smile comes on my face, my heart rate picks up, and my mind pictures beauty in its purest sense.

In our culture today, we tend to idolize the rich and famous, irrespective of their manner, character, and integrity. Interestingly, Jesus gave great value to the potential of various individuals who were relatively unknown and were certainly not high on the status and popularity scales. I guess the lesson here is that it's relatively unimportant what name is given to us as a baby. However, it is extremely important that we live in a way that will bring honor and appreciation to the name that we have worn during our lifetime in

God's world. This doesn't mean that we cannot ever make mistakes or even fail in our efforts. It does mean that we do not give up or fail to get up when we fall. Some of the folks I most respect are sinners who have been forgiven, and they now carry the name Christian at the top of their credentials. I want my name to be written in the Book of Life, and when the roll is called up yonder, I'll be there.

Think on this: to guard your name, you must guard your mind and your heart.

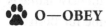
O—OBEY

O: Why is it so important to *obey*?

> *Children, <u>obey</u> your parents in everything, for this pleases the Lord.* (Colossians 3:20)

Obedience is so important in life. That's probably why it's so critical to begin learning it as a baby. None of us can remember exactly when we were first required to obey instructions. But remembering when Grammy and I first started to make rules for our children and then watching them teach their kids to obey is still vivid in my mind. No doubt there is a learning curve and some progress faster than others; a few may even revolt rather than comply. Let's give some thought to why submitting to authority is so necessary and important.

So much of life is spent interacting with others. For example, as babies, we become an immediate member of a family. Then all kinds of formal and informal groups of which we become a part begin to emerge. First, there are nurseries, schools, churches, clubs, teams, and even friend groups, to name just a few. I remember watching the first game of soccer played by two six-year-old beginner teams. It was fascinating. For most of the game, all that I observed was a group of boys moving around in a tight bunch on the field. I never saw the ball, which was somewhere among them. Toward the end of the season after the rules of the game were learned and followed, what a difference! Some goals were scored and games won, unlike their first contests that ended zero to zero.

As we grow older, we begin to understand why there are some rules and standards in various groups, organizations, and institutions. Without them, probably little or nothing would function properly and chaos would be the result. In our communities where we live, rules and laws are in place to ensure public safety and order. In all of these, obeying and following these decrees are keys to the quality of life there. All these are important, but there is another command that supersedes them all.

In the early books of the Bible, there were many orders and directives given to God's people. Unfortunately, many of these were ignored and/or disobeyed. All were actually designed and directed for the good of his people. This all changed when Jesus came to earth and brought a new covenant. He told us that there are certain commands that are greater than others, and if we will obey the two most important ones, the other necessary ones would follow. You probably remember these: first, love God, and second, love your neighbor (others). He is specific about this. "This is how we know that we love the children of God; by loving God and carrying out His commandments. This is the love for God: to obey His commandments" (1 John 4:2-3).

Think on this: trust and obey, for there's no other way to be happy in Jesus than to trust and obey.[7]

🐾 P—PRAYER

P: By nature, I'm a talker, so why was saying a *prayer* so hard for me at first?

> *Do not be anxious about anything, but in everything,*
> *by <u>prayer</u> and petition, with thanksgiving, present*
> *your requests to God.* (Philippians 4:6)

I've decided that the act of praying has to be learned; it's not something that comes naturally. And it takes practice to become comfortable with doing it. I remember knowing two prayers when I was growing up. "Now I lay me down to sleep; I pray the Lord my soul to keep" and "God is great, God is good, let us thank him for our food" were the extent of my prayer repertoire. When I looked up the definition of *prayer*, words like *request* (for help), *expression* (of thanks), and (reverent) *petition* kept coming up. These are all good, but I wondered if there were some other words that might be helpful in enhancing my practice of praying.

In thinking about this, my mind starts focusing on some of my closest relationships with others. There are some in my family and circle of friends who I just enjoy being with. For some reason, there is a strong, intimate, and meaningful connection that draws us together. If asked to cite just one factor that makes these relationships so strong, I think it would be this: *we truly love and care about each other.* As we interact, communication and sharing seem to come so easy and naturally. Would something like this be helpful in enhancing my practice of praying?

I have several acquaintances that seem to be very comfortable when asked to lead in prayer. One is my brother-in-law, whose prayers are not much different from when he's having a conversation with me. Another is a youth director who grew up in a small, rural community. When he prayed, it was like him talking to me on the phone. He would tell who was calling and get right into what he was calling about. I guess what has impressed me most about these and some others is their prayers seem so authentic yet personal.

Early in my life, I hardly ever prayed. If asked to pray at some event, I would write it down and read it verbatim. Growing up around preacher types who were so eloquent in their prayers, I felt inadequate and uncomfortable when praying publicly. But over time, the strangest thing happened. Like my relations with good friends, my growing relationship with God's Son, Jesus, gradually tore down the barriers and my inhibitions that separated us. I learned conclusively that God truly loves and cares for me—so much that he gave his Son that I might have life. The only thing lacking in the relationship was for me to do my part. So with prompting from the Holy Spirit, I fell in love with God. And as a result, my prayer life is alive and well today. I look forward to the time Grammy and I share in prayer each morning before we start our day. When asked to pray for someone, I always do so right then. I don't want to forget it. I'm not much of an orator when praying publicly, but I'm sincere. But the best part of my prayer life is what goes on during all my waking hours. I talk with him about everything—request for help, expression of thanks, and reverent petition. If asked to cite just one factor that makes this relationship so strong, I know it would be this: *we truly love and care about each other.*

Think on this: prayer is more than spoken words; it's a relationship between you and God.

🐾 Q—QUIET

Q: This is another letter with few options. I chose *quiet* because it's one that I sometimes struggle with.

> *He leads me beside quiet waters, he restores my soul.*
> (Psalm 23:2–3)

In some older versions of the Bible, instead of *quiet,* the word *still* is used, such as with "still waters" in the Twenty-Third Psalm. These two adjectives carry the same message, but I sort of like quiet better. I guess it's because today we live in such a loud world, and as a result, quiet time is hard to find. It's been interesting to me to observe some kids as well as adults who need to be busy all the time. Evidently, their energy levels or hyped psyche drives them and hinders them from sitting still. My mother used to tell everyone, "Bernie has to have a project, and he always wants someone with him." I'm better now, but Snookie often reminds me that I still have that tendency.

We live on Happy Valley Lake that is shared with seven other families; we moved here almost thirty years ago. It's a little less than a hundred yards down to the lake in our backyard. At every opportunity during our first years, I would hurry down with my rod and reel and tackle box in great anticipation of catching a mess of fish. Then one afternoon several years later, I was home alone with some issues at work weighing heavily on me. I decided to walk down to the lake and just sit on the dock. The wind had died down and the surface of the lake was like glass. The sun was beginning to set over the dam at the other end, and the reflection of the trees with their fall leaves was breathtaking. I sat there for a long time taking all this in. On the way back up to the house, I realized that something special had occurred. The weight was not nearly as heavy and my strength to carry it felt renewed.

Over the years, this experience has been repeated many times, and now sometimes Snookie and I together will go down to the lake in the late afternoon and observe the artistry and beauty of God's handiwork. It is not by accident that when "He leads me beside quiet waters, He restores my soul."

Think on this: I've heard more good things when it's quiet than when it's loud!

THE GOSPEL ACCORDING TO ST. BERNARD

🐾 R—RIGHTEOUS

R: Just because I think that I'm right doesn't mean that I'm righteous.

The <u>righteous</u> will live by faith. (Galatians 3:11)

Righteousness is not a subject that I feel qualified to say much about because I often feel that I fall far short in this area. Some folks believe that being righteous is the requirement for an abundant as well as an eternal life. However, to be truly righteous, a person must act right, think right, and even have right motives while never doing anything wrong—all the time. I could possibly live up to that standard for five minutes. But this doesn't mean that we should not seek righteousness for our lives.

When I was the CEO of a large health system, I always wanted to do things right. But more times than I would like to admit, something got in the way or I just messed up, particularly in the early days. There were times that I felt like I had done the right thing, yet it turned out to be the wrong thing. And on the other hand, I remember some instances when I actually did the wrong thing yet things turned out all right. I guess that over time, I began to realize that nobody's perfect in this area of righteousness. And to complicate things even more, I found out that sometimes what I think is right is actually wrong in the mind of others. And also there are many situations where there might be no pure right or wrong. Are you as confused as I am? So how do you resolve this quest for righteousness?

First of all, when faced with decisions, who defines what is right and what is wrong? As you get older, you begin to realize just how little you know about things in this world. The complexities are endless in certain facets of life. This reminds me of the futility of a doctor trying to treat a patient without knowing the diagnosis.

The Bible gives us guidance in this area. It points out that some insist on pursuing righteousness through works—like being under the law. In other words, in order to have the right relationship with God, we must earn it by proving ourselves worthy. If you look at this from a worldly perspective, that is probably the prevailing belief. But God's Word is very specific in regard to this when it states,

> For it is by grace you have been saved, through faith—
> and this is not from yourselves, it is the gift of God—not
> by works, so that no one can boast. (Ephesians 2:8–9)

This says to me that righteousness is not to be our goal in itself. But it can be ours only by God's grace though our faith.

Think on this: righteousness is not earned (works); instead, it is a gift (grace) from God to us that accompanies our belief (faith) in him.

🐾 S—SEEK

S: This letter offers many worthwhile possibilities, but finally I settled on *seek*.

> But <u>seek</u> first his kingdom and his righteousness, and all
> these things will be given to you as well. (Matthew 6:33)

To me, *seek* means trying to get something, usually for myself. Many of you may be like me; my main seeking is for success in an endeavor that has my focus at a given time. The definition of success for me in this context has changed over time. Looking back, at first, I was probably seeking those things that satisfied my needs. Then success grew into getting things that fulfill my wants.

And unfortunately, all this becomes contagious: the more I get, the more I want.

I would like to make a confession here. I've been a professional seeker all my life. Over the years, my efforts have revealed themselves in many areas, including material possessions, titles and status, social acceptance, meaningful relationships, security, and even health and lifestyle issues. The game of life, as I call it, has been a continuous journey of seeking to find those things that I believed would bring success or victory. This may sound self-centered and maybe even egotistical, but looking back, I don't believe that such efforts are inherently wrong or evil.

Now having lived out much of my life here on earth, I can view all of this from a broad perspective. I have no regrets toward being a passionate seeker. I truly believe that it is what God intended for us as we search for purpose and meaning in our lives. My only regret is that I had not discovered earlier to seek first God's kingdom and his righteousness. If I had, all the other things would be mine as well. Not necessary what I wanted but instead what I really needed to live a truly successful life. This revelation has not led to my doing anything different but to do the things that I was doing differently.

Think on this: what you truly seek you usually find, so make sure that you're looking in the right places and for the right things.

🐾 T—THANKS

T: I chose *thanks* because it is one of those words that originates in the heart but is delivered by the tongue.

> Give *thanks* to the Lord, for he is good. His love endures forever. (Psalm 136:1)

Saying thanks is a learned activity. I believe this because when I was young, my mother and daddy reminded me over and over to say thank-you when someone gave me a gift or a compliment or even opened a door for me. For some reason, it just didn't come naturally. The effect of an expression of gratitude like this didn't really hit home to me until I saw and felt it from the receiving end.

I remember one instance many years ago that made me think how important and meaningful a simple thank-you can be. I was in early elementary school and my teacher decided that it would be a great idea for us to make something for our mothers for Christmas. We were given several choices, so I decided to paint a picture for Mom. I drew a duck and painted it with watercolors, and it was put in a small frame. To be honest, even then I didn't think that it was all that good; you had to use your imagination to recognize it as a duck, but I did my best. On Christmas morning, Mom opened the present, which was the first one that I ever had given her that was not store bought (selected with the help of my dad). She just sat there for a minute and then said, "Oh Bernie, thank you so much. It's the most beautiful duck that I have ever seen." I can't tell you how good and important that made me feel. It hung on her den wall for the next fifty years, and she would share with friends, "Bernie painted it for me when he was little."

After the many years that I've been around now, I'm convinced that you can't use this special word of gratitude too often. Last year, Grammy, while doing her morning devotional, started writing notes in a journal. She got the idea from a book entitled *One Thousand Gifts*. On the cover, concerning the author, it states, "Ann Voskamp discovered in giving thanks for the life she already had, she found the life she's always wanted."[8] In her journal, Grammy's handwritten words acknowledge the gifts from God for which she is so thankful. Some are big, some are small, and some were gifts that she didn't recognize initially that turned out to be blessings.

To be honest, I can't imagine someone coming up with a list of one thousand gifts. I just looked at the journal. Her last entry recorded today was 1,206.

Could I come up that many? You bet I'm going to try, and I'm starting with the gifts (blessings) of eight grandchildren and one great-grandson. Thank you, Lord, for Lindsey, Alex, Jordan, Noah, Nathan, Greta, Amanda, Brittany, and Ollie.

Think on this: Count your blessings and then thank God from whom all blessings flow, for he is good. His love endures forever.

🐾 U—UNDERSTANDING

U: I have a bad habit of sometimes misunderstanding true understanding.

> *We know also that the Son of God has come and has given us <u>understanding</u>, so that we may know him who is true.* (1 John 5:20)

When I hear the word *understanding*, my thoughts go to other words like *comprehending, interpreting,* and *grasping*. Some of the folks I know feel that they must understand something before they can believe or accept it. In the health care field where I spent my professional career, it was so difficult for me to understand complex diagnosis and treatment processes as well as ever advancing technology, medical devices and equipment, information systems, etc. that are part of large health care system. Even if I had been able to grasp it all, in just a few years, much of this would be obsolete due to new innovations. Everything seems to be on the move and constantly changing. Some assert that everything is changing except death and taxes. I guess these questions arise: How can one have true understanding in a changing world? Is there anything that does not change?

I have often used the illustration about the hospital in which I worked the longest: Kennestone Hospital in Marietta, Georgia. It is named for two mountains that it sits between: Kennesaw and Stone. When viewing these from the top of the hospital building, one will note that Kennesaw Mountain is covered with trees and vegetation that change with every season. On the other hand, Stone Mountain is basically a large rock that maintains its gray demeanor. I believe that life is much like this. There are things that are ever changing, and there are things that never change.

In a broad context, understanding this principle can serve us well. In my view, truth is one of those things that never change. Some might take issue with this by believing that truth is constantly evolving to fit society's changing morals and standards. Interestingly, a term that is used to describe something that is unquestionably true is the *gospel truth*. And remember that gospel means "good news."

Maybe the lesson in this is that *understanding* is the ability to distinguish between those things that are ever changing and those that should never change and not get them mixed up. Good news! Good news! Those things of the world are ever changing, and those things of God are never changing. And maybe we need some help in understanding this. *Trust in the Lord with all your heart, and lean not on your own understanding; in all your ways, acknowledge him, and he will make your paths straight.* (Proverbs 3:5–6)

Think on this: understanding is not only an excellent trait but a gift from God.

 V—VICTORY

V: When and how can we claim *victory* in our game of life?

> *He gives us the <u>victory</u> through our Lord Jesus Christ.*
> (1 Corinthians 15:57)

Like most boys growing up, I tried many sports, and in my case with very little success. My main bright spot in my athletic pursuits occurred toward the end of my first quarter in life—my last two years in college. I was a member of the first tennis team at Valdosta State College. In those days, it was a very small school. Despite our "new kid on the block" image, we won the conference title our first two years of existence. Looking back, I can vaguely remember the individual losses and victories during those years. But receiving the conference title is ingrained in my memory. That experience has let me to believe that true or ultimate victory comes at the end of the season.

My own life experiences have been much like my tennis career. I have certainly had my share of wins and defeats, both personally and professionally. My losses generally were the source of my down and discouraging periods, while my wins lifted me up and raised my confidence and spirit. Looking back, the outcomes of my battles were often due either to my own readiness or to my unpreparedness, to my strengths or to my failings. But certainly there also were occasions when external forces ultimately determined the verdict. I guess the point in all this is to emphasize that life is full of opportunities and challenges that can result in personal wins or losses.

This has been going on since the beginning of time. Using the Bible as a historical reference, all the characters recorded in it made mistakes that led to defeat. No, that's wrong; there was one who lived perfectly. His name was Jesus, but he certainly had an advantage in that he was the Son of God. But despite that, Jesus also lost his share of earthly battles. Yet at the end of the season, he won not only the battle but also the war that he was sent to fight.

At the end of our individual seasons, the goal is to win the trophy. Interestingly, there is only one match that will determine the outcome, and it is fought within us. It's a spiritual battle that requires a life-changing decision on our part—to believe. To believe this: *"For God so loved the world that he gave his one and only Son, that whoever believes in him shall not perish but have eternal life."* (John 3:16)

Victory!

Think on this: without experiencing defeat, victory would have little value.

🐾 W—WISDOM

W: As I approached the end of the alphabet, I began to wonder if I had anything else to add. Then *wisdom* came to mind.

> *The fear of the Lord is the beginning of <u>wisdom</u> …*
> (Psalm 111:10)

It is interesting to me that the Bible is full of instructions to "fear not!" Yet in this particular verse of scripture, we are told that fear is "the beginning of wisdom." Could it be that there is more than one kind of fear?

To me, wisdom is a wonderful attribute to have. I know people who I would describe as wise. They just seem to have special insight into life and what it's all about. I was asked to give the eulogy at a friend's funeral recently. He had been one of our organization's board members for many years and therefore was one of my bosses. In my closing remarks about this special man to a full sanctuary of family and friends, I shared the following: "I truly valued his *wise* counsel and holy example." I believe that wisdom is something that we all desire to have in our lives' resumes.

But what is *wisdom,* and how do you get it? It involves being knowledgeable plus having the ability to use that knowledge in such a way as to be of value to yourself and others. Words like *good sense, good judgment, awareness, being informed* and *understanding* are components of wisdom. And I think of wisdom being directed toward knowing and doing "good." If this is something that we really want and seek, where do we start? The Bible states, "The fear of the Lord is the beginning of wisdom …" We usually think of fear as a dreadful feeling, something frightful, dangerous, and alarming that we should resist. However, in this context, this isn't the kind of fear that we're talking about. Here, we move into a different dimension of *fear.* This word also means respect, awe, and reverence for something or someone. Yes! There are different kinds of fear. Maybe the key to acquiring wisdom is relatively simple. Embrace with utmost respect, deep reverence, and great awe those things that are God's. *In a true sense, fear of the Lord overcomes fears in the world.* In the words of the current generation, "He's got my back!"

Annette, my mother-in-law, once told her daughter, my wife, that she had married a "wise man." When Snookie shared this with me, I viewed it as one of the greatest compliments that I had ever received. I felt that she was exaggerating, and I'm still trying to live up to her kind description. Now I know how!

Think on this: those who realize that they are not as smart as they think they are, are wise.

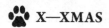 X—XMAS

X: There aren't many words that starts with the letter *X* in the English language, but I share *Xmas* with you.

> *Do not conform any longer to the pattern of the world,*
> *but be transformed by the renewing of your mind.*
> (Romans 12:2)

I don't remember this being used much lately, but Xmas is the abbreviation for Christmas. In researching this, I discovered that this originated through Greek interpretation and not from a secular attempt to remove the religious significances of this special day. Irrespective of this, to many of us who profess to be believers, we feel that there is a growing effort in our culture to remove Jesus Christ from society. Seemingly, the business and commercial sector in general loves the Christmas season because of its economic impact. Some of these enterprises as well as government and educational institutions have marginalized its origin by designating it "the holiday season" in the name of political correctness. Unfortunately, a growing number of our citizens no longer identify themselves as Christians or live as such. They are conforming to the patterns of the world. In some cases, even churches are also conforming rather than fulfilling their transforming mission.

Before this manuscript can be released for publication, the editors will x out those portions they believe are unnecessary or distracting. There is a great lesson here: we do need to remove many things from our lives that are unnecessary, but Jesus Christ is not one of these.

Think on this: Christmas without Christ is like celebrating a birthday without a birth.

 **Y—YOKE**

Y: I wanted to learn more about a *yoke*. I only recall seeing one a couple of times.

> Take my yoke upon you and learn from me, for I am gentle and humble in heart, and you will find rest for your souls. For my yoke is easy and my burden is light. (Matthew 11:29–30)

One of my neighbors has a yoke hanging near the entrance of his house. I viewed it as a relatively rare antique that was placed there as a conversation piece. A yoke is a wooden bar or crosspiece that connects two animals like oxen that plow a field. I surmised that the coupling of the animals keeps them pulling in the same direction as well drawing on the collaborative strength of the two. Working together in concert allows them to do together what they could never do alone and in a sense lightens the load of each.

This makes me remember an experience that I had many years ago. I loved to bird (quail) hunt. I was invited on a hunt with Mr. Harley Langdale, for whom the College of Business at Valdosta State University is named. The Langdales lived out from town surrounded by several thousand acres that were a part of his company. He was an avid sportsman and hunter and had all the amenities available for quail hunting. Included was a wagon for the hunters to ride, which also had pens for the dogs in the back. It was great to ride in it pulled by two matching mules that were joined by a yoke. However, the second time I visited, the wagon was not available because one of the mules had broken a leg. Usually when a mule or horse fractures a leg, its productive life is over. But I was told in this case, because these two animals had worked together for so long, an attempt was being made to rehabilitate the injured one. I went over and observed it in the stall with a cast on one leg.

The next year, I again visited for a bird hunt. With the two mules yoked and ready, we boarded the wagon again and enjoyed a great day of hunting. Mr. Harley told us about the healing process and the reuniting of the mule team. At first, the healthy mule had to carry a larger share of the load. But very soon, the recovering one began to show signs of growing strength and determination. Before too long, they were back in full stride, accomplishing what they were born to do.

The Bible verse above makes reference to us being yoked to Jesus. Can you imagine having someone always right beside you pulling life's loads? And as a result, your burden is lightened and you can find rest for your souls because he is the Son of God.

Mr. Harley Langdale became a very good personal friend whom I admired immensely. He was a great businessman and philanthropist. And he knew the real purpose of a yoke.

Think on this: One of our children once wrote this about Grammy and me: "They make an incredible pair, yielding higher results in their life together than either could have produced alone." I would add, "Being yoked to Jesus was the key."

🐾 Z—ZEAL

Z: Here, like a few other letters, choices are limited; however, I have a good one: *zeal*.

> *Never be lacking in <u>zeal</u>, but keep your spiritual fervor, serving the Lord.* (Romans 12:11)

I know a few people who seem to have an abundant amount of zeal. One is my very special wife, Snookie, whom our grandchildren call Grammy. She is full of energy and enthusiasm related to almost all aspects of her life. Her greatest focus in this regard is her family.

If a call or text comes to her phone from one of our children, and especially a grandchild, she immediately lights up, a big smile comes on her face, and excitement is in her voice. Unless there is a compelling reason limiting it, I know that it's going to be a while before she'll be available to me. I love it because, you see, I'm the person most often on the receiving end of her zealous caring spirit.

Interestingly, the verse from Romans cited above is in a section of the Bible about love. It talks about being devoted, joyful, patient, faithful, and practicing hospitality. All of these are ways to express love. In Snookie's conversations with those special to her like our grandchildren, I see love being demonstrated in the most intimate way. What is even more special about my wife's caring spirit is that it is also being exhibited constantly with others with whom she comes in contact. Today it was a waitress at the restaurant, yesterday it was a nurse in the doctor's office, and tomorrow it will be a visitor at church. One of our grandchildren told her one day, "Grammy, you like to talk to everybody."

Living with a zealot can be challenging, but in my case, it's worth tenfold and more. I'm learning from my wife how to keep my spiritual fervor, serving the Lord by loving others.

Think on this: be a zealot for the Lord, who zealously loves you.

This marks the end of my lessons to you on the *ABC's of Life*. This is the gospel according to St. Bernard.

CHAPTER 3

Pappy's Will and Testimony

This chapter is not about my last will and testament, which tell my desires to handle and distribute the assets of my estate after I'm gone. Instead, I want to offer to you a few additional thoughts concerning my *will* (desire for your life) and my *testimony* (sharing personal discoveries with you).

Growing up as a PK (preacher's kid) and always living in a parsonage (owned by the church) can give a kid a unique perspective of life. In my growing-up days, they used to say PKs, particularly sons, would turn out either very good or very bad. I think that this was because we were expected to be perfect and our behavior directly reflected our parents' relationship with God. What a burden this could be, at times resulting in rebellion by some. In my case, looking back, I viewed this much differently. We moved every four or five years to a new appointment and I immediately was connected with a new, large family—a church. To this day, I still have friends from each of those parishes where my father served.

I have another confession that I need to share with you about my past. In this little book, I'm attempting to offer you some helpful knowledge and wisdom from the standpoint of a grandfather to his grandchildren. I may not be the most qualified person to do such a thing, because I never had a granddaddy. Both my mom's and dad's fathers had died before I was born. Even though I didn't have my own personal role model in this regard, I have seen so many outstanding grandfathers in action who have filled this void. And I guess this is one reason that I feel so passionate about doing everything in my power to help each of my "grands" to find the key to an abundant and eternal life that is available to them.

I have attempted in the previous chapters to convey a whole lot of ideas and thoughts in regard to my mission to share "good news" with you. I close this effort with the following discoveries that have positively impacted my life.

🐾 LIFE IN SIN OR IN THE SON

I truly wanted my last little book to be upbeat and positive, but for some reason, I believe that this subject needs to be included. It is the main thing that erodes or even destroys the life that God has planned for us. So let me do my best to share my deep, heartfelt beliefs on this most difficult yet crucial subject: *sin*.

The definition that I believe best describes sin is this: Sins are the thoughts, motives, attitudes, and actions that separate us from God. They can grow and thrive in the earthly as well as in the spiritual realms (worlds). For this reason, an understanding of sin is very important; it is deadly and destructive in the greatest sense.

It was probably in my late thirties when I began seriously considering the ramifications of the real cost of sin. This came not in a time of crisis but during good times. My life had gone so well. I have the most beautiful and loving wife that I could imagine, wonderful kids who seem to get it, and a professional career that far exceeded anything that I had ever contemplated. I was immersed in work and civic and community activities, a member of the country club, and an active church leader. And in addition, I had accumulated more stuff than I could ever use. What else could I want or need? *I was living my way.*

Despite a good life like this, something seemed to be missing. My perceived calling lacked some of the things that I felt should accompany this level of success. I later identified the basic problem: there was a *gap between my career path and my faith journey.* Thankfully, a wonderful church with its spirit-filled staff, members and programs helped me gain the correct perspective to reevaluate the direction in which I was traveling. This helped me bridge that gap and led to a new purpose for my life, which involved turning the control over to God. I had many years earlier accepted Jesus Christ as my Savior and recommitted to this decision several times. However, I had only given lip service to making him Lord, which included not only my personal but also my professional life. A lay witness mission weekend that I attended resulted in my specifically making that new commitment. As a result, my job became my ministry. I didn't even have to do anything different, but I did have to do what I was doing differently. A new level of purpose, peace, and fulfillment accompanied this crucial decision. To the best of my ability, *I began living life God's way with his guidance.*

In looking back, I never thought of myself as a bad person. But through my own negligence, apathy, and self-centeredness, I had constructed a barrier or separation between God and me. This experience helped me to look at sin differently. I now view my greatest sin as "lukewarmness," which is as bad or worse than any others. *"I know your deeds, that you are neither cold nor hot … so because you are lukewarm, I am about to spit you out of my mouth."* (Revelation 3:15–16).

There can be a fine line between a life in sin and one in the Son (Jesus, the Son of God). There is only one letter difference in the two words—*i* and *o*. Sin has an *inward*, selfish focus; Son is *outward* focus on others. We all make choices every day.

My will is for you to make choices to live in the Son.

THE GOSPEL ACCORDING TO ST. BERNARD

🐾 STAKE IN THE GROUND

Critical, life-changing decisions are important, but even more critical is remaining true to those commitments. Unfortunately, I found myself off-track and even at time forgetting and questioning my earlier actions. This happens more often than many Christians like to admit. Then one day, someone shared with me a simple way to remind us who and whose we are. He worked on a farm that had a big barn on the property. To help him remember important times in his life, he would carve a date and message on a stake and drive it into the ground behind the barn. This always was there to serve as a reminder.

Another close friend had made his commitment to the Lordship of Jesus the same night that I did. So I decided to make us both a stake with a date routed on it. I had a little barn-shaped shop in the backyard at the time. I drove the stake into the ground and periodically visited that holy spot. I stopped by Jack's office one day and saw his stake hanging on the wall as a continuous reminder. We moved a couple of years after that, so I decided to hang mine on the wall also.

Interestingly, in addition to a stake being a wooden post with a sharp point used to give support, there are some other definitions. Stake can mean a share in something—like a stakeholder—and can describe something that can be gained or lost. All these meanings have application to the importance of staking our claims and honoring commitments in our lives that have eternal value. Since I hung my stake on the wall, I have never doubted my commitment to life in the Son.

My will is for you to stake a claim on the truly important plans God has for you.

🐾 NEW INVESTMENT STRATEGY

When Grammy and I took our stand to follow Jesus, we felt a need to make changes in many aspects of our lives. One of these was in regard to our investing strategies. We invest with our time, moral support, prayers, fellowship, hospitality, and all the other means of sharing and caring for others. However, the area that was most affected by our decision was how we would invest our financial resources—our money. Since we were married, we always have been members of a church, and from the beginning, we pledged and paid a tithe (10 percent of our income) to our church. If we gave to other organizations or charities, this would be additional. Our total income during our first year was $1,800 or $150 per month. The rent for our one-bedroom apartment was $75 per month, so we had the balance of $75 for living expenses. Our monthly tithe was $15, but for some reason, we pledged $5 per week (or $21.67 per month). Amazingly, we never missed a meal or ran out of expense money during the entire year.

The next forty years, which took us to retirement from my health care career, were unbelievable. The blessings of a family, home, job, community, and church have greeted us at every turn. There, of course, were challenges, opportunities, successes, failures, and all the other aspects of life. Worldly success in our society usually brings affluence, which raises the appetite for more, which in turn leads to temptation. Thankfully, with God prompting, we recognized this early on and thus began our commitment to properly manage our resources. One of the decisions that we made was that Grammy would stay home during the time our children were in school. I have always been so proud of her. She perfected the profession of homemaking and has been an advocate for it ever since.

During this time, we had four sacred principles we pledged to uphold. First, we would continue to tithe and support our church and other related agencies; second, we would not increase our basic standard of living as income grew; third, any major investments that we would make would be without significant debt. Fourth, we committed to embrace hospitality as part of our family mission to share ourselves and our possessions with others.

Having worked my entire professional career in hospitals and serving on boards of other nonprofit organizations, I saw firsthand how much charitable giving meant to their success in serving others. In this, we have observed the blessings that flow to those who give and share, and as a result, this has led us to expand our investment strategy. Today, we give priority to investing in those institutions, programs, missions, and ministries that have "eternal value." And thankfully, we have more to invest. We still haven't missed a meal or run out of expense money.

My will for you is that you will prosper in the important things of life and have a generous investment strategy in those things that have eternal value.

🐾 FAMILY MISSION STATEMENT

My first real job was in a grocery store. I worked there in junior high, senior high, and college. I started as a bag boy and worked my way up to being a butcher. After completing graduate school to prepare for a career in health care administration, I enjoyed my forty years career in six different organizations before retirement. And additionally, I have consulted or served on the boards of many others. I learned many things in each of these situations, but one principle has been ingrained in me regarding what makes an organization or institution truly successful. I found in all my experiences, some bad, some good and others better, organizations need to have a well-defined purpose or *mission*. And the team (employees, managers, executives, and board members) needs to understand and support it. Over and over, this proved to be a key ingredient for success.

To me, one of the greatest and most important organizations that exist in our society is the *family*. Its role is crucial to not only the success but maybe the survival of the human race. Today the absence of and/or dysfunction in families are the basis of more of our cultural problems than we would like to admit. If it is essential for other organizations to state their purpose, could this most important institution, the family, be well served to define its mission? In the Brown family, we are making an effort to address this. Below is our first attempt. I see it evolving and changing and being refined from time to time, but I believe that the basic principles will remain true. This was a team effort, and we have pledged to make our best efforts to fulfill it.

THE BROWN FAMILY MISSION

TO CREATE A FAMILY ENVIRONMENT WHERE:
- ONE CAN FIND REST AND BE RENEWED;
- RELATIONSHIPS CAN GROW AND FLORISH EVEN AMONG THOSE WHO MIGHT VIEW THINGS DIFFERENTLY;
- ENCOURAGEMENT CAN OVERCOME DISCOURAGEMENT;
- PEACE IS FOUND IN THE MIDST OF THE STORMS OF LIFE;
- BLESSINGS ARE REALIZED BY SHARING AND SUPPORTING OTHERS;
- UNCONDITIONAL LOVE ABIDES; AND
- JESUS CHRIST IS LORD.

We, the members of the Brown family, commit our best efforts to fulfill this mission that we have established together and encourage those who follow us to do likewise:

Snookie and Bernie Brown   *Jenny and Marc Bailey*

Susan and Jeff Brown   *Amanda and Brad McLean*

Est. 2018

My will is for your mission to be aligned with God's purpose for your life.

🐾 BUT FOR FOUR INCHES

In regard to my journey as a Christian, I have one more story to share with you. This occurred a while back so you may not have heard or just forgotten it. About two months before my retirement, a large, dead pine tree fell and struck my back as I was attempting to get out of the way. It fractured my scapular (one of the strongest bones in the body). I was in the hospital overnight and in a sling for six weeks. But the significance of this trauma that resulted from my own negligence was the report from the ER physician and orthopedist. They indicated in a very serious manner that if the tree had hit me just four inches to the left, I would be either dead or paralyzed. While I was in the hospital, my son-in-law came over and removed the fallen tree so I would not see it when I came home. Fortunately, today I experience very few physical repercussions from all this. Actually, after a few months of getting back to normal, this experience began to fade in my mind, even though initially I felt extremely lucky. But this is not where the story ends.

I was not one who claimed that God had spoken directly to me. Actually, I have often been leery of a few people I've known who have made such a pronouncement. But one night, I had a dream about the accident; it was so realistic and was just as I remembered. But there was one difference. When I arrived home from the hospital, I felt a real need to return to the site of the incident. I guess this was sort of like getting back on the horse after being thrown. In the dream, the fallen tree had not been removed by Brad. I stood looking at the tree that had broken apart into two pieces; one lay on the top of the other, forming a cross. I felt that I was standing on holy ground. Then the most amazing thing happened. I heard a voice that distinctly said, "I died for you so you could live for me."

When I woke up, I began to think back to all the details that I could remember. I even checked the day that this happened and realized that my dream occurred exactly ten years from my night in the hospital. Even today, only a few have heard the rest of this story, and I am a bit leery myself sharing it. Sometimes I think that it was just a dream, but then I realize that God has also spoken to many others in dreams. I'm a different person today, when I remember *but for four inches* that I might not even be here to share my stories with my grandchildren. I'm truly blessed.

My will for you is that you will be alert to God's voice.

God loves you, and I love you too.

This is the gospel according to St. Bernard.

CHAPTER 4

Your Life and Decisions

If this book were a novel, this would be the chapter where the mystery is solved. And if it were a how-to manual, this is the point where the answers to life's riddles would be revealed. But unfortunately, I can neither solve the mystery nor answer the riddles because we are all different and unique. God made us that way. We each were created on purpose for a purpose and "are fearfully and wonderfully made in his image." Therefore, we must work out our own personal relationship with him. However, just because the mystery isn't yet solved and the manual is without specifics, this doesn't mean that we can't explore some helpful ideas.

Looking back on what we have covered, it seems that much of life falls into two main categories. One is the natural and the other is the spiritual or, stated another way, the worldly and the heavenly. We can't escape the fact that we live in this world; however, this doesn't mean that there isn't another place in which we can also claim residence. For a limited period, we hold dual citizenship. In the big picture, our actual stay on earth is *very* short, whereas our heavenly residence will have no end.

Thinking back during my early and even teenage years, I gave very little thought to heavenly or eternal things. The earthly challenges seemed to fill most days. I do remember at a point feeling like I ought to believe this religious stuff because my dad was a preacher. But as I began to explore, it became even harder to understand. Could all this about Jesus being the Son of God and coming down to the earth to save us from our sins be true? At first, I doubted it but began to wonder, *What if it is true and I missed my ticket to heaven?* I remember deciding that I had better hedge my bets and at least profess to be a believer. I even became sort of an evangelist who wanted to have it both ways. In spite of my somewhat schizophrenic spiritual state, I now see that some important seeds were planted which geminated and later resulted in good fruit. I wish that I had been more perceptive and receptive to God's will and purpose for my life back then.

At this point, I'm asking each of you, my grandchildren, to step out of your comfort zone and think about what your life is all about. What do you feel will be the really important and maybe critical decisions that you will face? Let me ask three questions, which hopefully will stimulate your thinking about this. Consider these both from a worldly as well as heavenly point of view. I believe that this can serve as a self-analysis exercise and be beneficial to all of you.

1. What are your top three priorities in life?

When I was interviewing candidates for key leadership positions in my organization, we would spend time talking about training and experience. Then just before finishing, I would ask this question, and I received all sorts of responses. You could see most of them trying to figure out what I wanted to hear. Some would try to make light of it in a witty or humorous way. Then I would attempt to bring them back to get a serious and honest answer. Of course, there were also some who were a bit devious; time proved that they did not practice what they professed. But what always impressed me most were those who opened up and shared from their heart, even if their priorities were different from mine. *What are your top three priorities in life?*

2. What is your definition of success?

Today, success is largely measured in terms of achievement in one's professional or vocational endeavors. Titles, power, prestige, money, and influence tend to be some of the adjectives describing those who are successful. I remember at my retirement party a lot of important people were invited and some said a lot of nice things. That evening as we drove home, I could hardly hold back all my feelings of pride and accomplishment. But was I truly successful? *What is your definition of success?*

3. How do you want to be remembered when you are gone?

I'm deep in the fourth quarter of life, and now my thoughts and even my purpose and goals are changing as I ponder this question. You may have heard the poem "The Dash"[9] by Linda Ellis. It's about looking at the tombstone on a friend's grave. There inscribed are the dates he or she was born and died. Between these is a dash that represents the time that that person was alive on earth. The poem talks about life between these dates and what is said about you at your funeral based on how you lived your dash. *How do you want to be remembered when you are gone?*

I have given these three questions a lot of thought, particularly in the past few years. It has become obvious to me that the answers are different when viewing them from an earthly versus a heavenly perspective. Therefore, I have to make a decision through which of these lenses will I look. No longer am I hedging my bets; instead,

THE GOSPEL ACCORDING TO ST. BERNARD

I truly believe that Jesus Christ is the Son of God and came down to earth to save us from our sins. And I accept him as my Savior and Lord. Based on this decision, these are my own answers to the three questions.

1. These are my top three *priorities* in reverse order. Third is my *job* (or work), second is my *family* (those whom I love), and first is *God* (creator, redeemer, and sustainer). In summary, I believe that the right priorities are the keys to success. The job provides a means of success, the family provides a reason for success, and God provides the way to success.
2. True *success* is not measured in terms of dollars, trophies, or titles but in the often unrecognized contributions one makes to others and the inner joy one experiences from following God's purpose for one's life.[10]
3. I want to be remembered (my dash) as a man who loved to love God and others. If I am such a man, I believe all the other memories of me that I desire will fall into place.

What decisions do you need to make about your life and future? There are too many to list, and if we tried, we would still unintentionally miss some. One of my friends years ago told me something that has helped me enormously in facing life's highs and lows and the in-betweens. He said, "If you can't know everything, it's important to know someone who does and depend on his help." I know that person who knows everything that was, that is, and that will be. His name is Jesus, and he is the Son of God. He died for me on the cross and left a Holy Spirit to constantly dwell in my heart. He doesn't always give me what I want, but he always provides what I need. He doesn't always remove danger from my paths, but he always walks with me. He doesn't always meet my timelines, but he always is there at the right time. He doesn't guarantee that my life will be happy, but he can bring joy into any situation I face. He doesn't prevent death, but he does give life. He said, "*I am the Alpha and the Omega, the Beginning and the End.*" (Revelation 21:6)

I have a bad habit of intruding into others' lives and telling them what they ought to do. Some of my fishing buddies ragged me incessantly on some of our fishing trips because of my unwanted opinions that I always offered. I am well-known by many who have experienced my constant response "Let me tell you what you ought to do." I mention this because my first instinct here is to tell you what I think you ought to do. But I refrain because something this important and crucial is very personal and is between you and God. All of you know of him, some of you know something about him, and some may truly know him. Remember that "if you can't know everything, it's important to know someone who does." What a friend we have in Jesus!

On the next page is a place to record your own answers to the three questions.

God loves each of you, and I love you too!

Pappy

This is the gospel according to St. Bernard.

THE GOSPEL ACCORDING TO ST. BERNARD

Your Answers to Three of Life's Important Questions

1. What are your top three priorities in life?

2. What is your definition of success?

3. How do you want to be remembered when you are gone?

CHAPTER 5

Summary and Conclusion

This has seemed like a long journey for me, and I know also for you who are still with me at this point. I've thought a lot about whether this effort has been worth it and, more importantly, if it is helpful to my grandchildren. I mentioned before that their ages range from early teens to early thirties; the average is just above twenty years old. Is it realistic for them to grasp what I'm trying to convey? Oh, me of little faith! With the finish line in sight, I had a discussion with each of them about this project, and to be honest, I was so impressed by their reaction and response. They all are on board. I guess that it's been so long since I was their age that I forgot how they too are searching for answers to life's questions. Actually, I'm a bit ashamed that I didn't give the credit that was due them. These young folks not only got it, but they seemed ready and willing to march into adulthood with enthusiasm and passion. It made me want to be young again.

In my Christian journey throughout my life, I have often wondered what I should be doing. So often the answer from God was "Share the good news." But how? One of the old adages you probably have heard that best describes folks' efforts in this regard is "They walk the walk and talk the talk." Another instruction that I often received was "Go and tell." Good news needs to be shared, and you will be amazed at the sharing opportunities that come your way. I would challenge you as I have myself. Look for those times, and be intentional in both walking and talking the good news messages. It is never too early to start and never too late to share some good news.

Let me close with one last experience that hopefully reinforces my grandchildren's future in God's world.

I just found in one of my older Bibles a copy of a letter sent to me by my cousin Billy Brown about twelve years ago. I had been searching for it for a while. Billy is the son of my dad's brother; our fathers have been deceased for many years. The letter was handwritten on notebook paper and was from my dad to his dad. It's fairly long, but I was so moved by its contents that I have saved it for these many years. I haven't changed anything from the original.

Tuesday Night, May 15, 1928

Dear Bill,
It is 7:30 by my clock, so I have decided to drop you a few lines before going into my studying.

This week is review week with us, so you may know that I've got to put out some hard studying. Our exams will start next Wednesday, May 23, and will end on Friday following. One week from next Monday is Commencement Day. It is hard to realize that next week is the last of school, but it indeed thrills me when I think about it. I still have hopes of passing all my subjects, except Latin. I'm right on the edge of flunking algebra, but I have made an honest effort if I do flunk it. I have hopes of passing it and think maybe I will. Last night I put about two (2) hours of hard studying on it. If

I flunk algebra, I'm sure I'll go home for summer school.

Bill, I have been thinking for some time that I would talk with you by letter about a question which I consider very serious. It is the question of religion. I know you are a good man, Bill, but there is always room for us to improve ourselves. I think you and I may be drawn closer to each other and closer to God if we discuss this matter together.

Religion consists not only in prayer; it means that the man who prays shall also keep his engagements with his fellow men to the minute; it means he shall use his money in the sight of God. That he shall be cheerful, chivalrous, dependable. It means that a man's conversation shall be truthful, kind, and wise. It means that his time shall be wisely planned out and used for useful ends. That his mind shall be concentrated, his thoughts marshaled under a domination purpose.

One sees people who seem perfectly sincere in their devotional life go straight out from it all into the engagements of the day without taking the Spirit or the mind of Christ with them. No one would dare say that those people are conscious hypocrites. The trouble is they are earnest largely on their inner side. They are the victims of a partial, broken view of religion. They have their beliefs right, but their beliefs do not get much of a chance to open their purses. They are faithful to their devotions but not to their appointments. No amount of devotion on the inner side of life can make up for the lack of it among the outward facts.

Do not think that I put more emphasis upon the life of action than upon the life of secret devotion, any more than I look upon the fruit of a tree as more important than the root. As it is impossible to get fruit from the trees without roots, so it is impossible to obtain Christian character without being rooted in the eternal realities which produce it.

There seems to be a terrible temptation to refuse to obey the spirit of God within us, when he urges us to go a step beyond the current standards and sentiments, which we find around us. We are willing to be Christians up to that point to which conventional opinion says we must do. But when that point is reached, we are tempted to refuse to go further—so that we become not so much obedient to the Spirit of God as to a certain social conscience.

The need of our time is for men who have the root of the matter in them to progress in Christian conduct beyond the frontier of conventional conception of duty, to continue to be obedient to the Spirit of God after they have reached what convention requires. For the Spirit of God has a long and progressive program for us all, which he reveals hour by hour and day by day, to all those who are willing to continue to carry the mind of Christ into individual and social life.

I want to recommend to you, if you do not already know him, a crucified Christ who is able to do anything. God has meant much and is still meaning much to me in my life. I try to live my religion, and I do live it the very best I know how.

I am very appreciative, Bill, for what you have meant to me. I appreciate the interest you have in me and the interest you take in Mother. God will reward you some day for your kindness.

I must get busy. Write me sometime. Rec'd Mother's cards (2) today, also rec'd a letter from Helen Brasington.

This leaves me okay and happy.

Lots of love,
Your devoted brother,
Bernard Loam[11]

To my grandchildren, this was written by your great-grandfather, who died before you were part of the family. You may have noticed that this was written on May 15, 1928. Dad was just completing his freshman year at Emory University, where he had just begun his educational journey in earnest. He was eighteen years old at the time, and I was amazed at his insight and maturity at that age. He grew up in a small, rural community in South Georgia, and this was the first time that he had been away from home. He was the first from his family to get a college degree. My take from this was that despite his relatively young age, he already had a strong relationship with the Lord. And he wanted to share it with others, especially with his older brother. Uncle Bill became a very successful businessman and was one of the nicest and most generous persons I have ever known. Dad, Bernard Loam Brown Sr., continued his college education through seminary and became a Methodist minister. I observed many folks, young and old, cry when he left their churches to go to another appointment. He was a pastor to many during his fifty-year career. In my mind, he wrote the first St. Bernard Gospel.

My point in including this personal story is it's *never too early*

THE GOSPEL ACCORDING TO ST. BERNARD

to begin your spiritual journey in earnest and to share the good news with others. And I again would add it's *never too late* to make one more effort to share something that might make a difference in someone else's life.

This is the gospel according to St. Bernard.

EPILOGUE

The Value of Old Folks

It's Wednesday, November 27, 2019, and I'm working on my book. I need to keep up the pace to complete it on the schedule that I have established for the project. Even though I'm not in the mood to be creative, I'm making an attempt to write something worthwhile anyway.

For some reason, I thought of my famous mother. She died more than seven years ago. If she were still living, she would now be over one hundred years old. I say she was famous because she was an author, having something published in the *Reader's Digest* almost forty years ago. It was one of those "Life in these United States" type stories printed at the bottom of a page. Let me share with you what it said.

Generation Raps

> We were dining at a restaurant with friends, and one of us said it might be interesting to turn back the clock and live one's life over again. I mentioned that I would like to be 18, but know what I now know. Our young waitress interrupted, saying, "I'm eighteen and what do you know?"
>
> – Contributed by Elizabeth Brown[12]

Mom's little story just as it appears here was cut out of the magazine and placed in a large frame with a wide mat. For years it hung with much pride on her den wall.

I sometimes think that none of my life stories shared with any eighteen-year-old would enlighten him or her all that much. This is mainly because much of the knowledge and the little bit of wisdom that I have accumulated have been gleaned from experiencing. And I doubt that I could ever adequately describe the thrill of my personal victories or the agony of my personal defeats. One can try to tell others about things like marriage, the birth of a son or daughter, the death of a parent, acquiring a job or losing one, a new car or an automobile accident, a good report on the annual physical, a heart attack, and on and on. However, words cannot come close to matching the actual experience of any events such as these. This attitude can lead to just keeping my thoughts to myself. Then I remembered so many of the lessons that my parents, grandparents, aunts, and uncles passed on to me through their stories and the way they lived.

It seems to me that one of the main advantages of getting older is that a tremendous amount of wisdom is gained from "experience." Old folks have a great deal to offer to us, and we need to take advantage of it. In past generations and even today in some cultures, the older a person gets, the more revered he or she becomes. Old people frequently "rule the roost" in their homes and communities. Their opinions are sought after and deferred to, and younger people actually look forward to aging because of the privileges it brings. Today, our culture has become more youth oriented, with an emphasis on physical appearance, accomplishments, and personal and professional status. As a result, we often relegate our older folks to the background, dismissing them as being "over the hill" when in fact they are treasuries of knowledge, wisdom, and understanding.

For a while now, I have been taking a more personal interest in this particular subject. For some reason, I feel like I'm becoming more philosophical, more flexible, more tolerant, more appreciative, and even wiser. Maybe this is due to the vast experience I have been accumulating, or maybe it's just because today, November 27, 2019, is such a big day. Today, I turn eighty!

To my grandchildren, I offer these final thoughts and observations. Thank you all for making me feel that you not only love me but you also value me. As you grow older, approach life with an inquisitive mind, a listening ear, a restrained mouth, a helping hand, and a caring heart. I believe that I know each of you pretty well, and I'm proud of what I see and observe. You will have wins and losses, highs and lows, satisfactions and disappointments and a lot of experiences between these extremes. That's life. But probably the most important thing to remember is that you are here for a purpose and in the end it's going to be all right. As the scriptures say, *"And we know that in all things God works for the good of those who love him, who have been called according to his purpose"* (Romans 8:28).

God loves you, God values you, and God cherishes you, and I do too!

Pappy

FAMILY ALBUM

Grammy is the photo album queen in our family. Remembering back, I believe that she started this hobby in earnest over fifty years ago with the birth of our first child. Her many albums are often looked at as a frame of reference. At some family events, they are placed out for viewing and reminiscing. But the most entertaining time is when our grandchildren look at pictures of their parents when they were young. Grammy usually writes in the album or on the back of each photo an identification of the people and the places. What a treasure all of these are to our family. Here, I will share a few glimpses of my beautiful family

🐾 MEET MY GRANDCHILDREN

Since the content of this book is directed primarily to my grandchildren, I thought it might be appropriate to introduce them to others who might read it. Of course, when a grandfather is given the opportunity to share stories about his grandchildren, he can go on and on. I'll try to be considerate and limit myself to one memory about each of them.

Lindsey is really pretty and is into a healthy lifestyle—diet, exercise, etc. She graduated from UNC Charlotte and is out in the work world. Lindsey was our first grandchild, and as such, we often tell her, "We don't love you more than our others, but we have loved you the longest!" Since Lindsey has been ours the longest, a special bond has developed between us, especially between Lindsey and Grammy. From the beginning, Lindsey had such a sweet spirit, but she also has very strong convictions in regard to her beliefs. It could be that these characteristics, which are similar to her grandmother's, are part of the reasons for their close personal relationship. It is not unusual for either one of them to text and set up a good time to have a telephone conversation. Grammy usually wants an update on her activities, and Lindsey will often ask Grammy's opinion on something she is dealing with. Sometimes, I hear one side of the conversation and marvel at the warm and deep relationship that these two family members have with each other. What makes this so special and even inspiring to me is that there are fifty-three years and two generations separating them. They usually end each call with something like this: "I love you more than the turkey roll-up that I had for lunch" or "I love you more than the cup of Starbucks coffee I have in my hand right now." I would add, "I love you both more than I can express on a sheet of paper in a book that I'm writing."

Alex (Alexandria) is also a beautiful girl. She just completed her freshman year in the Business School at Auburn University, where she pledged Zeta Tau Alpha Sorority. She loves family traditions. For example, she and Grammy have decorated the angel tree in our foyer each Christmas for as long as I can remember. My favorite memory concerns a project that Alex collaborated on with her great-grandmother (Elizabeth Brown). Alex's middle name is Elizabeth. "Grandmama," as she was called, wrote a children's book when she was ninety years old. Alex was eight at the time and has some artistic talent. So Grandmama asked her if she would draw the illustrations for the book. The name of the book was *Who I'd Like to Be*, and it includes a poem about a little boy who wondered what it would be like to be something else: a bird, pig, cow, duck, etc. Alex's brother was five at the time so I think that she could identify with the book's message, and she did a great job with her drawings. Grandmama called and wrote several notes to Alex thanking her and telling her what a great job she did. A little while later, Grandmama (my mother) shared a note that she received from Alex. It said, "Dear Grandmama, thank you for your call and letters; the words were good too!"

THE GOSPEL ACCORDING TO ST. BERNARD

Jordan is a good-looking guy. All the girls think so, and I agree because one of our relatives told me that he looks a lot like me at that age. Jordan will be a sophomore at Georgia Tech and has plans to be an engineer. He followed in his dad's footsteps in both engineering and running. Jordan was a cross-county athlete in high school. He's also been very helpful to me. I remember him pruning bushes, spreading pine saw, and splitting wood for me and a neighbor from fallen trees after a storm.

When he was in the second grade up in Louisville, Kentucky, you could already tell that he was smart. He came home one day after school and told his mom that he had "figured it out." He said, "It's not that hard. All you have to do is do what you're told and you won't get into trouble." His mother, Amanda, was impressed and says that by and large Jordan practiced what he preached. Interestingly, a few months ago, just before he left to go off to college, Grammy shared this little story with him. His response was "I don't remember that, but I wish that I had!"

Noah is the athlete in our family; he loves every sport that has a ball. He's a competitor who played football, soccer, golf, lacrosse, and baseball, and one year, he was even in a fishing club. He will be a senior at Mt. Paran Christian School. A few years ago when he was in middle school, we were watching one of his basketball games. It was one of those where his team took control early using a full-court press against the opponent. Noah was a guard, so he very often stole the ball and had a lot of easy layups. Actually, in the third quarter, the outcome of the game was basically decided. The coach started substituting, and before long, Noah was the only starter still in the game. He continued to steal the ball, but instead of scoring more on easy opportunities, he started feeding the ball off to the new players who had entered the game. The game ended up a rout, and what impressed me most wasn't the fact that Noah was the leading scorer but what the coach shared with the team as they gathered for the postgame review. He said, "Men, this was a great team effort. Every player on the team scored and contributed." I was standing close enough to hear, so I looked over at Noah and smiled and winked.

THE GOSPEL ACCORDING TO ST. BERNARD

Nathan just completed his first year in high school. He is a couple of years behind due to a valiant battle he fought with neuroblastoma. This is a rare but severe form of pediatric cancer with which he was diagnosed when three years old. The disease and side effects of the treatment caused some damage to his body, but his mind and spirit exhibit the strength of a victorious warrior. He may be physically small, but spiritually he is a giant. His life has been an inspiration to hundreds and maybe thousands who have followed his story for the past thirteen years. Many of these have been his prayer partners.

Three years ago, the Dominion Christian School that Nathan attends began a fundraising program to support childhood cancer research with the Rally Foundation. He became the driving force behind this initiative, which he along with his mother has led each year. In addition to the internal efforts to raise support, a football game played during Pediatric Cancer Awareness Month also highlights the program. Thousands of dollars have been raised through these efforts.

Each year, Nathan has served as an honorary captain of the football team and flips the coin to begin that game. This past season, he also began traveling with the team and became a ball boy assisting the referees. Because so many have followed Nathan's story, I have become famous. Today, I'm known most often as "Nathan's granddaddy."

THE GOSPEL ACCORDING TO ST. BERNARD

Greta is the one we call our "song and dance girl." Since she was very young, she has enjoyed performing. She just completed her final year in middle school and already is a veteran of many musicals, concerts, recitals, and choral programs. In addition to singing, she plays the piano and French horn and is an accomplished dancer. We have been so impressed with her performances on stage over the years but have been even prouder of some of her off-stage decisions and activities. She has always been friendly toward the lonely.

She is our youngest grandchild, so you can probably imagine how special she is to us. She is so pretty, so cute, so smart ... In any production, my first thought is that she would be great as the beautiful female heroine or leading lady. But Greta generally doesn't want that type of role. Instead, she auditions for what I would call a "character role." As examples, she has played Sebastian (the crab in *The Little Mermaid*); Pugsley (the son in *The Addams Family*), etc. Interestingly to me, even though her beauty is usually hidden under an unflattering costume, her personality and talent are exhibited in a humorous, a touching, and/or a powerful manner. She brings joy to the audiences in such roles.

Amanda, after receiving her college degree and working for a short time, married Nathan Ward. In my estimation, they fit together perfectly. Some even say they favor each other enough to be brother and sister. Just over a year ago, they were blessed with their first child: a son they named Oliver (Ollie). Amanda and Nathan are great parents and just fun folks to be with. We've enjoyed several events and cookouts at their home.

Amanda is a people person; she is witty, outgoing, and caring. She has been very active in rescue programs for animals and dogs especially. She and others who were encouraged by her have adopted dogs and provided good homes for them. Her caring, giving, and serving passion was exhibited in a different way recently. For Ollie's first birthday party, she asked that children's pajamas be given to a local charity to be used for needy children instead of a gift for Ollie. Even though her son is too young to understand all this, she wanted from the beginning to train him to recognize the blessings of giving to others.

The two highlights of our relationship with Amanda and Nathan were attending their wedding and being present for Ollie's baptism—two very sacred and holy events.

THE GOSPEL ACCORDING TO ST. BERNARD

Brittany is an artist—a performing artist. As a professional dancer, she is very interested and committed to applying her training and skills while expanding her horizon to help improve the lives of others. She is very independent, driven, and passionate about making a positive contribution. Currently, Brittany is a junior at Columbia University and focusing on a multidiscipline course of study.

One of my favorite recollections concerning Brittany occurred a while back. She was taking a very demanding course in which the professor, due to an unexpected conflict, was forced to leave before the end of the semester. The students were informed of this and told not to worry about their grades and all would receive full credit for the course. Unlike others who were delighted to be done and get a good grade, she was very disappointed with this decision, feeling that she would not be adequately prepared for other courses that would follow. So after she expressed objections to no avail, Brittany decided to complete the course on her own. This evidently impressed some of the faculty to the extent that new opportunities have come her way—assisting in teaching some courses and managing some laboratory activities. This really amazed me too, because there is no doubt that I would have been in the camp of the grateful to escape the rigors of a tough course.

Ollie (Oliver) is our first great-grandchild and as cute as they come. He recently celebrated his first birthday. Amanda Ward, his mother, is a dog lover extraordinaire and is actively involved in rescue programs for them. Currently, three dogs (Cavalier King Charles spaniels) reside at the Ward home and are a prominent part of the family. So Ollie has never known a home without his canine buddies. It has been interesting to watch his growth and development during his first year. To me, he seems on schedule with all the benchmark activities expected of a one-year-old. Since he and his family live in Hickory, North Carolina, we haven't been able to see him very often. However, I was a little concerned about one thing. He loves his furry friends and they love him. The dogs have many toys and even a little inside house in which they play. Ollie seemed to enjoy most being a part of the pack; I guess crawling on all fours is something like running on four legs. I never shared this, but I was a bit concerned that he might think that he was a dog. However, the last time we were visiting Hickory and saw Ollie, all my fears disappeared. He had taken his first steps and was walking; he was jabbering instead of barking and even saying, "Mama" and "Dada."

THE GOSPEL ACCORDING TO ST. BERNARD

🐾 FAMILY PHOTOS

Snookie and Bernie, 1962.

The original Brown family, 1975.

Amanda Bailey and Nathan Ward's wedding, 2017. Lindsey, Amanda, and Brittany.

The Jeff Brown family, 2019. Alex and Noah.

The McLean family, 2019. Jordan, Nathan, and Greta.

The Brown family at Christmas 2018.

Family at Bernie's eightieth birthday, 2019.

The Granddogs

The Wards and Baileys

The Jeff Browns

The McLeans

Brittany Bailey

NOTES

1. Brown, Bernie. *Purpose in the Fourth Quarter* (Bloomington, IN, Inspiring Voices, 2012) p. 78.
2. Feiler, Bruce. *Reader's Digest*. (New York, NY: Trusted Media Brands, Inc.) September 2013, p. 34.
3. C. Stanley. *In Touch*. (Atlanta, Georgia: In Touch Ministries, Inc.) November 10, 2019, p. 30.
4. Yancy, Philip. *Reaching for the Invisible God*. (Grand Rapids, MI: Zondervan, 2000). p. 251.
5. Newton, John. "Amazing Grace." Public domain.
6. Bobby McFerrin. "Don't Worry Be Happy." (ProbNoblem Music) 1988.
7. Sammis, John Henry. *Trust and Obey*. Public domain.
8. Ann Voskamp. *One Thousand Gifts* (Grand Rapids, MI: Zondervan, 2010) cover.
9. Ellis, Linda. *The Dash*. (Southwestern Inspire Kindness, Inc. 1996–2018).
10. Brown, Bernie. *Lessons Learned on the Way Down*. (Bloomington, IN, Inspiring Voices, 2010) p. 121.
11. Letter reprinted with permission of the W. C. Brown Sr. family.
12. Brown, Elizabeth. *Reader's Digest*. (New York, NY: Trusted Media Brands, Inc.) August 1984, p. 132.

Books by Bernie Brown*

Lessons Learned on the Way Down: A Perspective on Christian Leadership in a Secular World

Purpose in the Fourth Quarter: Finishing the Game of Life Victoriously

Snookie and Bernie Are Sweethearts: An Anatomy of a Marriage (coauthored with Bernie's wife, Snookie)

Road Signs on the Journey Home: Fifty-Two Modern-Day Proverbs

Adventures of the Bass Buddies: Tales of Fun, Folly, Friendship, Faith, and a Little Fishing (coauthored with three friends)

All are available at Amazon.com/books and other booksellers Bernie's email address is bernielb@bellsouth.net.

*All proceeds benefit educational, healthcare, community and church organizations and institutions.